Hard Core

Defeating Sexual Temptation with a Superior Satisfaction

Jason Hardin

DEWARD
PUBLISHING COMPANY

Hard Core: Defeating Sexual Temptation with a Superior Satisfaction
© 2010 by DeWard Publishing Company, Ltd.
P.O. Box 6259, Chillicothe, Ohio 45601
800.300.9778
www.dewardpublishing.com

Cover design by Jonathan Hardin.

Unless otherwise noted, scripture quotations are taken from The Holy Bible, English Standard Version®, copyright ©2001 by Crossway Bibles, a publishing ministry of Good News Publishers. Used by permission. All rights reserved.

Any emphasis in Bible quotations is added.

Reasonable care has been taken to trace original sources for any excerpts and quotations appearing in this book and to document such information in the endnotes. For material not in the public domain, fair-use standards and practices were followed. Should any attribution be found to be incorrect or incomplete, the publisher welcomes written documentation supporting correction for subsequent printings.

Printed in the United States of America.

ISBN: 978-0-9819703-8-7

Honesty about our successes is one thing. Honesty about our failures and shortcomings is quite another.

*This work is dedicated to those brothers and sisters who have been a refreshment to my soul by being transparent and authentic in their walk with God. You are models of the motto that means so much to me: **esse quam videri**. You know who you are. Thanks for being you and for helping me along the way.*

contents

1. Introduction 7

2. Casualties of War 11

3. The Reason for Everything 17

4. The Cold, Hard Stats 23

5. "It Was Very Good" 37

6. God's Warning Signs 43

7. A Time to Fight, and a Time to Run 49

8. Frustration Sets In 61

9. Even Those After God's Own Heart
   Can Be Devoured 65

10. Counting the Cost 71

11. God's Steadfast Love is Better Than Life 75

12. The Fruit of a Broken and Contrite Heart 85

13. It's Time to Walk Down Another Street 89

14. Hacking Agag to Pieces 93

15. Equipped for the Battles Ahead 99

Notes 105

one

Introduction

I had already written this Introduction. I had moved on to other parts of this book. In fact, the final draft was nearly complete.

Then I got the e-mail. Five days before this manuscript went to the printer, this is what landed in my Inbox:

> Jason,
>
> I'm reaching out to you as a Christian man who is caught in the snares of sin, but is unable to free himself. I feel as if there is nobody I can talk to, for various reasons. I heard you speak recently, and I've read *Boot Camp*. I've been a Christian for well over 15 years, attending church since I was born. I know the gospel message. I know I can't escape on my own, but only through God's help will I win every man's battle. Yet here I am—still caught.
>
> This is an anonymous plea for help, but you can call me "John."

This sort of plea could be duplicated thousands and thousands of times over. "John" is by no means alone. I've received a shocking number of similar pleas in recent years. What you hold in your hands is my best attempt—at this point in my walk with Christ—to convict, encourage, and strengthen people who know exactly what "John" is talking about.

With those goals in mind, this is a straightforward little book. It is straightforward because so many—men *and* women included—are being slaughtered in their struggle with sexual sin. The spiritual carnage is everywhere, and it continues to mount. Individual lives, marriages, children, friendships, influences for good, ministries of gospel preachers, and entire congregations of the Lord's people are being seriously impacted by compromises and losses in the battle against sexual immorality. It is commendable for us to sing, "Soldiers of Christ arise and put your armor on." But if we sing those words, then proceed to ignore, cover up, soften, gloss over, or downplay where the battle is being lost in the lives of so many, the devastation will only continue to grow.

And so this is a straightforward little book about an uncomfortable topic. It is uncomfortable because so many—men *and* women included—don't quite know how to address what must be addressed. Different people handle the discussing of this difficult topic in differing ways. Let me say from the outset that I am not looking to offend anyone. I take Paul's charge in Colossians 4.6 very seriously—"Let your speech always be gracious, seasoned with salt, so that you may know how you ought to answer each person."

At the same time, I know there will be men and women of all ages who would read right over softer, less poignant, more vague terminology and fail to fearfully appreciate the present danger. Much worse, I know that some would fail to see themselves and their desperate need to repent of their sins.

When I am ensnared by sin, I do not need you to pat me on the back. I do not need you to commend me, then walk away. I do not need those who care about me to act as if nothing is wrong.

When I am in bondage to iniquity, I need to be lovingly and firmly brought face to face with God's truth. I need to be stopped in my tracks and rebuked, as David was by Nathan. I need to feel the weight of those words, "You are the man!" And then I need to be shown, through clear transmission of God's will, how to address and conquer what is separating me from my heavenly Father.

If we are going to help men and women of all ages win this battle, we must strike at the root of the problem. We must unashamedly examine God's boundaries. We must call sin, sin. We must sound the call for righteous warfare. We must encourage our beloved brothers and sisters in Christ to be "steadfast, immovable, always abounding in the work of the Lord, knowing that in the Lord your labor is not in vain" (1 Cor 15.58). We must dedicate ourselves to hard-core holiness.

By all means, let's continue to sing, "Soldiers of Christ arise." But let's also be fearfully honest with ourselves. Let's be sure to truthfully and lovingly convict men and women about the gaps in their armor and equip them so that they might win the battle against sexual immorality and glorify our heavenly Father in the process.

As I wrote in the Preface of *Boot Camp: Equipping Men with Integrity for Spiritual Warfare*, I am no expert. I'm an ordinary guy who is tempted just like you. I've compromised just like you. I've sinned just like you. My only qualifications for writing this material are a passion for the Savior and an earnest desire to encourage my fellow soldiers on the battlefield. The challenge of writing this pales in comparison with the task of practicing what I'm preaching. But I have also tasted and seen that the Lord is good! (Psa 34.8).

I pray that our heavenly Father will use these words

of a recovering sinner, saved by his grace, for your good. I pray that you will be driven a little closer by something in these pages to the superior satisfaction that is available in him.

To him be the glory. Great things he has done.

Core Questions

1. Can you relate to "John's" e-mail?

2. "I feel as if there is nobody I can talk to." Have you ever felt that way before? What backs people who are "caught in the snares of sin" into this kind of a corner?

3. Why is it vital that we talk straightforwardly about sexual temptation?

4. How have you seen people ignore, cover up, soften, gloss over, or downplay this topic? Why do people do those sorts of things?

5. What role should passages like Colossians 4.6 play in discussions of temptation?

6. In your own words, what will "hard-core holiness" look like?

two

Casualties of War

My family and I recently visited some of the Civil War battlefields in Maryland and northern Virginia. They don't really look like battlefields any more. The grass is green and well-manicured. The trees are tall and full of life. The surrounding hills have long recovered from the scars of war. The legendary generals of the past have been replaced by polite tour guides. Forts have given way to souvenir shops. The only competition that remains is over parking spots. Tourists armed with cameras and students on field trips are the only people who roam these fields today. In most cases, long-impotent canons and weathered marble statues are the only indicators that you aren't walking through a typical State Park that was set aside for family picnics and disc golf.

It is relatively easy for a bored teenager to scan these open fields and completely miss the point. Preoccupied parents with restless children in tow can take a few moments to glance over the countryside and leisurely walk away, unmoved by the history of these hallowed grounds. But these fields have been carefully preserved for a reason. They are the sites of the struggles of the deadliest war in American history. An estimated 620,000 people lost their lives on and around these serene, now peaceful fields. That number exceeds the loss of life in all other American wars from the Revolution through Vietnam.

September 17, 1862 produced the single bloodiest day in American combat history. The Union and Confederate armies met in the Maryland farm fields bordering Antietam Creek near the town of Sharpsburg. From dawn until dark, the two armies relentlessly threw frontal attacks at each other, littering the ground with their dead and wounded. "The whole landscape for an instant turned red," one northern soldier later wrote. Another veteran recalled, "[The cornfield] was so full of bodies that a man could have walked through it without stepping on the ground." All told, an estimated 23,000 men were killed in a matter of hours—more than twice as many as in the War of 1812, the Mexican War, and the Spanish-American War combined.

No clear victor emerged that day, and the fighting stopped only out of sheer exhaustion. General Robert E. Lee and his troops withdrew across the Potomac River under the cover of darkness. Tactically speaking, the battle ended in a draw.[1]

While you live in a time far removed from the American Civil War, you cannot afford to ignore that you are engaged in a conflict over your soul that will never end in a draw. As an image-bearer of God, you are confronted with an Enemy who never sleeps. "Resist the devil, and he will flee from you" (Jas 4.7), but live long enough, and he will return. As long as this world stands, he will never surrender. As long as souls are in the balance, he will never stop scheming. Attacks from all angles will continue, and he is not alone. "For we do not wrestle against flesh and blood, but against the rulers, against the authorities, against the cosmic powers over this present darkness, against the spiritual forces of evil in the heavenly places" (Eph 6.12).

As you make your way through the battlefield of life, the spiritual landscape is absolutely littered with downcast and defeated souls. Men and women. Young and old. More are being taken captive as prisoners of the awful struggle every hour.

This war is being waged on many different fronts, but surely one of the hottest and fiercest is the flank of sexual integrity. In fact, it may be the single bloodiest and most vulnerable weak spot of our time. The problem is, so many people—Christians included—cross the plains of sexuality more like they are taking a leisurely stroll through a State Park than waging war across a field of battle. The rules of civilized conduct are simple. Mind your own business, don't bother your fellow picnickers, and clean up after yourself.

Most any addiction counselor will tell you about the "motto of dysfunction."

Don't talk, don't trust, don't feel.

Individuals buy into that motto. Marriages are maintained according to that motto. Families are raised with that motto. Entire congregations limp along for decades in unspoken agreement with that motto.

All the while, as we diligently work to maintain respectable false fronts and show off our attractive hypocritical masks, the Enemy is leading a shock-and-awe campaign against the core of character. While we are picnicking and faking our way through life, our inner beings are withering. While we offer lip-service and feigned reverence for God, our hearts are hardening, our consciences are searing, our integrity is being butchered, and our souls are being carried to the eternal fire prepared for the devil and his angels.

"Don't talk, don't trust, don't feel" may be the unspoken motto for an unhealthy culture, but it is not the motto for true followers of Jesus. Secret sin is a horrible thing, and a wake-up call is desperately needed. To be caught can be absolutely gut-wrenching. But one thing is even worse—never being caught, holding ourselves unaccountable, until we stand before King Jesus in judgment. "For God will bring every deed into judgment, with every secret thing, whether good or evil" (Ecc 12.14).

Our Risen Lord did not hide or sugarcoat the toll this war for our souls can take.

> "You have heard that it was said, 'You shall not commit adultery.' But I say to you that everyone who looks at a woman with lustful intent has already committed adultery with her in his heart. If your right eye causes you to sin, tear it out and throw it away. For it is better that you lose one of your members than that your whole body be thrown into hell. And if your right hand causes you to sin, cut it off and throw it away. For it is better that you lose one of your members than that your whole body go into hell." (Matt 5.27–30)

It's hard for me to imagine what it would be like to live life without one of my eyes or one of my hands. But Jesus wants me to recognize that something vastly more critical is at stake. There is something more serious even than losing a right eye or a right hand, and it centers around my heart—the core of my identity.

> "What comes out of a person is what defiles him. For from within, out of the heart of man, come evil thoughts, sexual immorality, theft, murder, adultery, coveting, wickedness, deceit, sensuality, envy, slander,

pride, foolishness. All these evil things come from within, and they defile a person" (Mark 7:20–23).

All the evil things that Jesus mentioned have a "supply line" that must be severed. It is the condition of my heart that will provide fuel for what I do with my body, whether good or evil. If I literally cut off my right hand and physically tear out my right eye, what good will that do if my heart remains rotten to the core? No, if I am to master what is continuing to defile me, the supply line of sin must be severed. This is an issue of the heart—and that's what this book is all about.

Core Questions

1. As you read Ephesians 6.12, what comes to your mind?

2. Why, if we resist the devil, will he flee from us?

3. What do you think about the "motto of dysfunction"— don't talk, don't trust, don't feel? Why is living by this motto so dangerous and destructive?

4. How do you feel when you read Ecclesiastes 12.14?

5. What should we make of Jesus' straightforward words in Matthew 5.27–30?

6. How can the "core" of someone's identity ever be reshaped? Where would such an improvement project even begin?

The Reason for Everything

You exist for a reason. It is **the** reason. Every thing in the universe exists for **this** reason. Are you listening?

You exist, according to the purpose of God's will, for the praise of his glory.

God made that truth abundantly clear to the descendants of Abraham through his prophet Isaiah in the Old Testament.

> But now thus says the LORD,
>> he who created you, O Jacob,
>> he who formed you, O Israel:
> "Fear not, for I have redeemed you;
>> I have called you by name, you are mine.
> When you pass through the waters, I will be with you;
>> and through the rivers, they shall not overwhelm
>>> you;
> when you walk through fire you shall not be burned,
>> and the flame shall not consume you.
> For I am the LORD your God,
>> the Holy One of Israel, your Savior.
> I give Egypt as your ransom,
>> Cush and Seba in exchange for you.
> Because you are precious in my eyes,
>> and honored, and I love you,
> I give men in return for you,
>> peoples in exchange for your life.

> Fear not, for I am with you;
>> I will bring your offspring from the east,
>> and from the west I will gather you.
> I will say to the north, Give up,
>> and to the south, Do not withhold;
> bring my sons from afar
>> and my daughters from the end of the earth,
> everyone who is called by my name,
>> whom I created for my glory,
>> whom I formed and made." (Isa 43.1–7)

Israel existed, according to the purpose of God's will, for the praise of his glory.

In the New Testament, the Spirit's message to Christians in Ephesus is much the same.

> Blessed be the God and Father of our Lord Jesus Christ, who has blessed us in Christ with every spiritual blessing in the heavenly places, even as he chose us in him before the foundation of the world, that we should be holy and blameless before him. In love he predestined us for adoption as sons through Jesus Christ, according to the purpose of his will, to the praise of his glorious grace, with which he has blessed us in the Beloved. In him we have redemption through his blood, the forgiveness of our trespasses, according to the riches of his grace, which he lavished upon us, in all wisdom and insight making known to us the mystery of his will, according to his purpose, which he set forth in Christ as a plan for the fullness of time, to unite all things in him, things in heaven and things on earth. (Eph 1.3–10)

You exist for a reason. It is **the** reason. Every thing in the universe exists for **this** reason.

You exist, according to the purpose of God's will, for the praise of his glory.

And so we ought not to be surprised at the kind of language we find in Psalm 148.

> Praise the LORD!
> Praise the Lord from the heavens;
>> praise him in the heights!
> Praise him, all his angels;
>> praise him, all his hosts!
>
> Praise him, sun and moon,
>> praise him, all you shining stars!
> Praise him, you highest heavens,
>> and you waters above the heavens!
>
> Let them praise the name of the LORD!
>> For he commanded and they were created.
> And he established them forever and ever;
>> he gave a decree, and it shall not pass away.
>
> Praise the LORD from the earth,
>> you great sea creatures and all deeps,
> fire and hail, snow and mist,
>> stormy wind fulfilling his word!
>
> Mountains and all hills,
>> fruit trees and all cedars!
> Beasts and all livestock,
>> creeping things and flying birds!
>
> Kings of the earth and all peoples,
>> princes and all rulers of the earth!
> Young men and maidens together,
>> old men and children!
>
> Let them praise the name of the LORD,
>> for his name alone is exalted;
>> his majesty is above earth and heaven.

He has raised up a horn for his people,
>   praise for all his saints,
>   for the people of Israel who are near to him.

Praise the Lord!

You exist, according to the purpose of God's will, for the praise of his glory. Practically speaking, you will fulfill the reason for your existence by being holy. "As he who called you is holy, you also be holy in all your conduct, since it is written, 'You shall be holy, for I am holy'" (1 Pet 1.15–16).

The angels praise God by serving as ministering spirits (Heb 1.14). The sun praises God by shining. The moon praises God by waxing and waning. The rain and snow praises God by falling. The wind praises God by blowing. The trees praise God by bearing fruit. The birds praise God by flying. And you exist to praise God as well! You exist to praise God by being a living representation of his holiness.

The obvious problem is, not one of us lives up to our calling. "None is righteous, no, not one; no one understands; no one seeks for God.... for all have sinned and fall short of the glory of God" (Rom 3.10–11, 23). Which is why God "has blessed us" with the gospel "in the Beloved. In him we have redemption through his blood, the forgiveness of our trespasses, according to the riches of his grace, which he lavished upon us, in all wisdom and insight making known to us the mystery of his will, according to his purpose" (Eph 1.6–9).

You exist, according to the purpose of God's will, for the praise of his glory. If you have been mercifully redeemed by the blood of Jesus Christ, obtaining the forgiveness of your trespasses, according to the riches of his grace, God's will for you is that every aspect of your life—your body, your heart, your soul, and your mind—would be united in him. God's plan all along has been "to unite all things in him, things in heaven and things on earth" (Eph 1.10).

Your charge, therefore, is transformation. Your goal is conformity. Your motto is to be, "My Father's will be done, in my life as it is in heaven."

> What shall we say then? Are we to continue in sin that grace may abound? By now means! How can we who died to sin still live in it? Do you not know that all of us who have been baptized into Christ Jesus were baptized into his death? We were buried therefore with him by baptism into death, in order that, just as Christ was raised from the dead by the glory of the Father, we too might walk in newness of life. (Rom 6.1–4).

You exist, according to the purpose of God's will, for the praise of his glory. You belong doubly to God. He created you and he redeemed you from your sins with the blood of his Son. Why, then, would you ever be content to continue living in the filth of immorality?

> Or do you not know that your body is a temple of the Holy Spirit within you, whom you have from God? You are not your own, for you were bought with a price. So glorify God in your body. (1 Cor 6.19–20)

The sad truth is, so many of us are continuing to compromise our holiness. We are being devoured by the Enemy of our souls on the front of sexual impurity. Don't believe me? The numbers are overwhelming.

Core Questions

1. This chapter repeatedly emphasizes, "You exist, according to the purpose of God's will, for the praise of his glory." In your own words, what does that mean?

2. 1 Peter 1.15–16 clearly states God's expectation of his image-bearers. Practically speaking, what does it mean for us to "be holy"?

3. Ephesians 1.10 states that God's plan is "to unite all things in him, things in heaven and things on earth." What will it look like if your body, heart, soul, and mind are "united" in God?

4. What sort of mottos have you lived by in the past? What about, "My Father's will be done, in my life as it is in heaven"? How would that motto change everything for the better?

5. Why would anyone reason within themselves, "Are we to continue in sin that grace may abound?" (Rom 6.1)

6. What do you make of 1 Corinthians 6.19–20?

four

The Cold, Hard Stats

Pornography and statistics seem often to go hand in hand. I'm confident that many readers of this book would be disappointed if this kind of chapter was not included. If surveys and statistics aren't of much interest to you, don't get lost in the next few pages. But do take the time to at least feel the weight of what is represented in this chapter. Some of the numbers are mind-blowing.

Compiling accurate statistics about sexual impropriety and the uses of pornography can be a daunting task. So many of the stats found on the Internet lack real context or an accurate citation of sources. That's why I was particularly impressed with a study released in January 2010 by Covenant Eyes.[2] Consider just some of the statistics from this extensive report.

Pornography and Profits
- In 1997, *US News & World Report* stated that adult entertainment was estimated to be an $8 billion industry. Adult Video News (AVN) estimated that the figure, even then, was $2 to $3 billion higher than the estimate.

- In 2005, the adult industry—including video sales and rentals, Internet sales, cable, pay-per-view, phone sex, erotic dance clubs, magazines, and novelty stores—made $12.62 billion.

- In 2006, the adult industry made $13.3 billion.

If those statistics are accurate, then the adult industry brings in more than the NFL, NBA, and Major League Baseball combined.

The Amount of Pornography on the Web

Damon Brown, author of *Porn and Pong* wrote,

It seems so obvious: If we invent a machine, the first thing we are going to do—after making a profit—is use it to watch porn. When the projector was invented roughly a century ago, the first movies were not of damsels in distress tied to train tracks or Charlie Chaplin-style slapsticks: they were stilted porn shorts called stag films. VHS became the dominant standard for VCRs largely because Sony wouldn't allow pornographers to use Betamax; the movie industry followed porn's lead. DVDs, the Internet, cell phones, you name it, pornography planted its big flag there first, or at least shortly thereafter.[3]

The National Research Council reported in 2002:

- 74% of commercial pornography sites displayed free teaser porn images on the homepage, often porn banner ads.

- 66% did not include a warning of adult content.

- 25% prevented users from exiting the site (this is called mousetrapping).

- Only 3% required adult verification.

In 2002, there were 100,000 adult websites based in the United States, and nearly 400,000 for-profit adult sites worldwide. In September 2003, the N2H2 database contained 260 million adult webpages—a near 20-fold increase since 1998. In December 2003, the Florida

Family Association provided an exhaustive report to the United States Department of Justice. Their special software program, *PornCrawler*, identified 297 million porn links (separate pornographic images) on the Internet. In 2004, there were 420 million webpages of pornography from nearly 1.6 million websites, 17 times greater than the amount registered in 2000.

One can only imagine the staggering amount of pornography available today.

Internet Porn Viewers

Paul Fishbein, founder of *Adult Video News*, boasted to the *New York Times*, "Porn doesn't have a demographic—it goes across all demographics."[4] Statistical research continues to prove that Fishbein is correct.

According to research done in 2008 by Kirk Doran, Assistant Professor in the Department of Economics at the University of Notre Dame:

- 14% of the online population of America visit adult websites and spend an average of 6.5 minutes per visit.

- 80% to 90% of these people only access free pornographic material.

- The remaining 3 million Americans who pay for Internet pornography pay an average of $61 per month; this generates $2.5 billion in annual revenues for the Internet porn industry.

The number one search term used on search engine sites is "sex." Online users search for "sex" more than the terms "games," "travel," "music," "jokes," "cars," "weather," "health," and "jobs" combined.

A 2001 Forrester Research report claimed that the average age of a male visitor to an adult website is 41; he has an annual income of $60,000. According to the same report, 19% of North American Internet users are regular visitors to adult content sites. Of that 19%, approximately 25% are women, 46% are married, and 33% have children.

According to Nielsen/Net Ratings, an estimated 34 million people visited adult entertainment sites in the month of August 2003—approximately one quarter of all Internet users in the United States. In September 2003, more than 32 million unique individuals visited a porn site. Nearly 22.8 million of them were male (71%), while 9.4 million adult site visitors were female (29%).

Internet Porn and its Effects on Marriage

A December 2009 press release from the American Academy of Matrimonial Lawyers reported the most prominent factors present in divorce cases:

- 68% of the divorces involved one party meeting a new lover over the Internet.

- 56% involved one party having "an obsessive interest in pornographic websites."

- 47% involved spending excessive time on the computer.

- 33% involved excessive time spent speaking in chat rooms.

In 2003, a Focus on the Family poll revealed that 47% of surveyed families said that pornography is a problem in their home.

The *Journal of Adolescent Health* warned in November 2009 that prolonged exposure to pornography leads to:

- An exaggerated perception of sexual activity in society.

- Diminished trust between intimate couples.

- The abandonment of the hope of sexual monogamy.

- Belief that promiscuity is the natural state.

- Belief that abstinence and sexual inactivity are unhealthy.

- Cynicism about love or the need for affection between sexual partners.

- Belief that marriage is sexually confining.

- Lack of attraction to family and child-raising.

The Internet, Pornography, and Teens

- According to an anonymous survey published in the *Journal of Adolescent Health* in August 2009, 96% of teens interviewed had Internet access, and 55.4% reported that they had visited a sexually explicit website.

- According to research from Family Safe Media, the largest group of viewers of Internet pornography is children between the ages 12 and 17.

- A study cited in the *Washington Post* in January 2007 suggested that more than 11 million teenagers view Internet pornography on a regular basis.

- In 2001, a study by social psychologists at the London School of Economics showed that 9 out of 10 children (ages 11 to 16) had viewed pornography on the Internet.

According to a 2008 survey of teens and young adults done by the National Campaign to Prevent Teen and Unplanned Pregnancy:

- 20% of teens have sent or posted nude or seminude pictures or videos of themselves.

- 39% of teens are sending or posting sexually suggestive messages.

- 71% of teen girls and 67% of teen guys who have sent or posted sexually suggestive content say they have sent/posted this content to a boyfriend/girlfriend.

- 21% of teen girls and 39% of teen boys say they have sent such content to someone with whom they wanted to date or "hook up."

Internet Porn and College Students

In 2009, Michael Leahy released the results of a survey of 29,000 college students at a variety of North American universities.

- 51% of male students and 32% of female students first viewed pornography before their teenage years (12 or younger).

- 35% of all students' first exposure was Internet or computer-based (compared to 32% from magazines, 13% from VHS or DVD, and 18% from Cable or pay-per-view).

- 42% of male students and 20% of female students said they regularly read sexually explicit magazines or regularly visited sexually explicit websites or chat rooms.

Porn at Work

- A 2003 study conducted by *Business & Legal Reports* suggested that 66% of the human resource professionals interviewed reported that they had discovered pornography on employee computers; 43% said they had found such material more than once.

- According to a study by *The Industry Standard*, 70%

of Internet porn traffic occurs between 9 a.m. and 5 p.m., when most people are at work.

• A 2005 study by computer science professors Maryam Kamvar and Shumeet Baluja (associated with Google) found that more than 20% of all mobile phone queries and 5% of personal digital assistant queries were searches for adult entertainment.

Pornography and Churchgoers

In 1994, a survey conducted by Word Publishing showed that 91% of men raised in "Christian homes" were exposed to pornography while growing up (compared to 98% of those not raised in "Christian homes").

In August 2000, *Christianity Today* conducted an exclusive survey of its readership on the issue of Internet pornography. Among those who classified themselves as "clergy," 40% had visited a pornographic Internet site, with more than 33% doing so within the last 12 months.

In 2003, *Today's Christian Woman* reported that 34% of their female readers admitted to intentionally accessing Internet porn, with 17% being regular users of pornography.

A 2006 survey by ChristiaNet, Inc. reported that 50% of men who would describe themselves as Christians and 20% of women who would describe themselves as Christians also acknowledged that they were addicted to pornography; 60% of the women who answered the survey admitted to having significant struggles with lust; 40% admitted to being involved in sexual sins in the past year.

In a 2008 cover story, *Christianity Today* reported that 70% of American men ages 18–34 view Internet pornography at least once a month. The same article warns,

Don't assume that porn isn't a problem in the church. One evangelical leader was skeptical of survey findings that said 50% of Christian men have looked at porn recently. So he surveyed his own congregation. He found that 60% had done so within the past year, and 25% within the past 30 days. Other surveys reveal that one in three visitors to adult websites are women.[5]

Pornography and Its Effects

Gary R. Brooks, Ph.D., describes a "pervasive disorder" linked to the consumption of soft-core pornography like *Playboy*. He mentions five main symptoms of this for men[6]:

- **Voyeurism** — *an obsession with looking at women rather than interacting with them;* this can apply to far more than pornography, including any consumption of the "sexuality-on-tap" culture in which we live; media glorifies and objectifies women's bodies, thus, promoting unreal images of women, feeding male obsession with visual stimulation and trivializing other mature features of a healthy sexual relationship.

- **Objectification** — *an attitude in which women are objects rated by size, shape and harmony of body parts;* sexual fantasy leads to emotional unavailability and dissatisfaction.

- **Validation** — *the need to validate masculinity through beautiful women;* women who meet centerfold standards only retain their power as long as they maintain "perfect" bodies and the lure of unavailability; it is very common for a man's fantasy sexual encounter to include a feeling of manly validation; it is also common for men to feel invalidated by their wives if they have trained their minds and bodies to respond only to the fantasy advances of their dream girl.

- **Trophyism** — *the idea that beautiful women are collectibles who show the world who a man is;* pornography reinforces the women's-bodies-as-trophies mentality.

- **Fear of True Intimacy** — *the inability to relate to women in an honest and intimate way despite deep loneliness;* pornography exalts a man's sexual needs over his need for sensuality and intimacy; some men develop a preoccupation with sexuality, which powerfully handicaps their capacity for emotionally intimate relationships.

On November 18, 2004, Dr. Judith Reisman, Dr. Jeffrey Satinover, Dr. MaryAnne Layden, and Dr. James B. Weaver were called to be witnesses before a U.S. Senate subcommittee on pornography. Here are some quotes from their statements:

- "There are no studies and no data that indicate a benefit from pornography use.... The society is awash in pornography and so, in fact, the data are in. If pornography made us healthy, we would be healthy by now." (Dr. MaryAnne Layden)

- "It has always seemed self-evident that pornography is nothing more than a form of 'expression.' ...Pornography is mere 'expression' only in the trivial sense that a fall from the Empire State building is a mere stumble—since it's hitting the ground that's fatal." (Dr. Jeffrey Satinover)

- "Modern science allows us to understand that the underlying nature of an addiction to pornography is chemically nearly identical to a heroin addiction." (Dr. Jeffrey Satinover)

- "Pornography triggers a myriad of endogenous, internal, natural drugs that mimic the 'high' from a street drug. Addiction to pornography is addiction to what I dub erototoxins—mind-altering drugs produced by the viewer's own brain." (Dr. Judith Reisman)

- "Pornography, by its very nature, is an equal opportunity toxin. It damages the viewer, the performer, and the spouses and the children of the viewers and the performers. It is toxic mis-education about sex and relationships. It is more toxic the more you consume, the 'harder' the variety you consume, and the younger and more vulnerable the consumer." (Dr. MaryAnne Layden)

- "The findings of numerous studies suggest that pornography consumption promotes sexual deviancy, sexual perpetration, and adverse sexual attitudes." (Dr. James B. Weaver)

A new study released in December 2009 by Patrick F. Fagan, Ph.D. (Senior Fellow and Director of the Center for Research on Marriage and Religion at the Family Research Council), examines the effects of pornography on individuals, marriage, family and community.[7] In the summary Fagan explains,

> Pornography is a visual representation of sexuality which distorts an individual's concept of the nature of conjugal relations. This, in turn, alters both sexual attitudes and behavior. It is a major threat to marriage, to family, to children and to individual happiness. In undermining marriage it is one of the factors in undermining social stability.
>
> Social scientists, clinical psychologists, and biologists have begun to clarify some of the social and psychological effects, and neurologists are beginning to delineate the biological mechanisms through which pornography produces its powerful negative effects.

Some of Fagan's key findings on the effects of pornography:

The Family and Pornography

- Married men who are involved in pornography feel less satisfied with their conjugal relations and less emotionally attached to their wives. Wives notice and are upset by the difference.

- Pornography use is a pathway to infidelity and divorce, and is frequently a major factor in these family disasters. Adults who steadily consume pornography are three times as likely to be unfaithful to their spouses.

- Among couples affected by one spouse's addiction, two-thirds experience a loss of interest in sexual intercourse.

- Both spouses perceive pornography viewing as tantamount to infidelity.

- Pornography viewing leads to a loss of interest in good family relations.

The Individual and Pornography

- About 25% of those who go on the Internet do so for sexual purposes.

- Up to 90% of youth aged 15 to 17 reported accidentally coming across pornography online. About one quarter of these youth said this happens "somewhat" or "very often."

- Many adolescents who view pornography initially feel shame, diminished self-confidence, and sexual uncertainty, but these feelings quickly shift to unadulterated enjoyment with regular viewing.

- Pornography is addictive, and neuroscientists are beginning to map the biological substrate of this addiction.

- Users tend to become desensitized to the type of pornography they use, become bored with it, and then seek more perverse forms of pornography.

- Men who view pornography regularly have a higher tolerance for abnormal sexuality, including rape, sexual aggression, and sexual promiscuity.

- Prolonged consumption of pornography by men produces stronger notions of women as commodities or as "sex objects."

- Pornography engenders greater sexual permissiveness, which in turn leads to a greater risk of out-of-wedlock births and STDs. These, in turn, lead to still more weaknesses and debilities.

- Child-sex offenders are more likely to view pornography regularly or to be involved in its distribution.

- The use of Internet pornography makes participants almost four times more likely to engage in paid sex.

Allow enough time for enough people to live and function in this sort of "pervasive disorder" and it is only a matter of time before you get the kinds of results the Barna Research Group reported in November 2003:

- 38% of adults believe it is "morally acceptable" to look at pictures of nudity or explicit sexual behavior.

- 59% of adults believe it is "morally acceptable" to have sexual thoughts or fantasies.

- 38% of adults believe there is nothing wrong with the use of pornography.

If you are struggling with these issues, I hope that the message comes through loud and clear—you are not alone. But miserable company, in and of itself, won't save you. You need God for that. And that leads us back to the very beginning.

Core Questions

1. Straightforward question: have you ever seen pornography?

2. If so, how were you first exposed to it, and how old were you at the time?

3. How many times have you seen it since?

4. When was the last time that you saw pornography? Did it "find you" or did you go looking for it?

5. Perhaps you have seriously struggled with this issue. Does what initially interested you or excited you about pornography continue to interest and excite you? Have your tastes for pornography evolved over time?

6. In all honesty, how has your heart been affected by sexual temptation in general? How has the way you look at members of the opposite sex been impacted? If you're married, how has your relationship with your spouse been affected by this issue?

five

"It Was Very Good"

God created sex. He created men and women as sexual beings. And what he created was very good. Genesis 2.15–25 documents the details for us.

> The LORD God took the man and put him in the garden of Eden to work it and keep it. And the LORD God commanded the man, saying, "You may surely eat of every tree of the garden, but of the tree of the knowledge of good and evil you shall not eat, for in the day that you eat of it you shall surely die."
>
> Then the LORD God said, "It is not good that the man should be alone; I will make him a helper fit for him. Now out of the ground the LORD God had formed every beast of the field and every bird of the heavens and brought them to the man to see what he would call them. And whatever the man called every living creature, that was its name. The man gave names to all livestock and to the birds of the heavens and to every beast of the field. But for Adam there was not found a helper fit for him. So the LORD God caused a deep sleep to fall upon the man, and while he slept took one of his ribs and closed up its place with flesh. And the rib that the LORD God had taken from the man he made into a woman and brought her to the man. Then the man said,

> "This at last is bone of my bones
> > and flesh of my flesh;
> she shall be called Woman,
> > because she was taken out of Man."

Therefore a man shall leave his father and his mother and hold fast to his wife, and they shall become one flesh. And the man and his wife were both naked and were not ashamed.

Tim Challies offers this theological reflection on God's good gift of sex[8]:

> God gives us sex because it has unique power in drawing a husband to his wife and a wife to her husband. He knows this because he is the one who invented it! He made it so that it is far more than the sum of its parts. We could describe sex in terms of body parts and hormones, but we would not be any closer to understanding it than if we were to describe a cake only in terms of its ingredients—flour and milk and eggs (or if we were to describe the Lord's Supper making reference only to eating bread and drinking wine). Sex goes far beyond merely the physical and instead extends to the emotional, the spiritual. It is through sexual union that two are made one, that they are bound together; there is a mystery to it that can only really be compared in impact to the union of God's people to God as they are grafted into him.

Isn't that why the apostle Paul referenced Genesis 2.24 in his often-quoted encouragement to husbands and wives in Ephesians 5.25–33?

> "Therefore a man shall leave his father and mother and hold fast to his wife, and the two shall become one flesh." This mystery is profound, and I am saying that it refers to Christ and the church. (verses 31–32)

God has blessed his image-bearers with a remarkably intimate and powerful gift. It is to be joyfully cherished and treated as a supremely special manifestation of God's glory and love. It is a shadow or type of a much greater reality. "Knowing" one's spouse in profound and mysterious ways foreshadows and deepens our appreciation for the greatest "knowing" of all—to know and be known by God himself. Marriage, Paul tells us, from the beginning of creation was designed by God to be a reflection of and patterned after God's relationship with his people.

The intimate nature of the husband-wife relationship provides a unique opportunity through which a man and a woman can grow to know one another, serve one another, express vulnerability to one another, give to one another and receive from one another. Our Creator was wise, therefore, to place clear warning signs all around his good gift. And he has every right to do so. He is the one who created it. Through his Spirit, he communicated to first-century Christians in Corinth that the physical aspects of the husband-wife relationship are to be enjoyed regularly throughout a marriage.

> Now concerning the matters about which you wrote: "It is good for a man not to have sexual relations with a woman." But because of the temptation to sexual immorality, each man should have his own wife and each woman her own husband. The husband should give to his wife her conjugal rights, and likewise the wife to her husband. For the wife does not have authority over her own body, but the husband does. Likewise the husband does not have authority over his own body, but the wife does. Do not deprive one another, except perhaps by agreement for a limited time, that you may devote yourselves to prayer; but then come together again,

so that Satan may not tempt you because of your lack
of self-control. (1 Cor 7.1–5)

When we use God's gift as God intends, we discover
great joy. There is no reason to be ashamed. We enjoy
beautiful freedom, mutual honor, and no defilement.
In fact, we will have strengthened our defenses against
Satan by using God's gift in the way God envisioned.

But when we neglect or abuse God's gift, immeasurable sorrow follows closely behind. When we know God's
will for our lives and our sexuality, but allow ourselves
to succumb to the alluring temptations of this world, we
have every reason to be ashamed. When we forget the
Giver of every good and perfect gift, and rebelliously de-
termine what is "good" and what is "evil" according to
our own moral compasses, we have already been warned
of the consequences.

For we know him who said, "Vengeance is mine; I will
repay." And again, "The Lord will judge his people." It
is a fearful thing to fall into the hands of the living God.
(Heb 10.30–31)

Core Questions

1. Why, in your own words, did God create sex?

2. What does the "one flesh" expectation of the Creator ex-
   pressed in Genesis 2.24 involve? Are the expectations pure-
   ly physical, or is more implied?

3. Why do you think Genesis 2.25 was documented by God?
   What ought we to take away from that statement?

4. In what way does Genesis 2.24 mysteriously and profound-
   ly refer to Christ and his relationship to the church?

5. The verb "knowing" is used in interesting ways in both the Old and New Testaments. What ought we to make of the use of that verb in Scripture? What is implied by its use when speaking in physical terms? What about in emotional terms? And spiritual terms?

6. How should 1 Corinthians 7.1–5 shape the married life of a couple and their expectations of one another?

six

God's Warning Signs

C.S. Lewis wrote, "The safest road to Hell is the gradual one—the gentle slope, soft underfoot, without sudden turnings, without milestones, without signposts."[9] And yet, if I travel that easy way that leads to destruction, I will not be able to feign ignorance, telling God that I had no warning. If I am separated from God for all eternity, it will be because I chose to ignore the signposts, acting as if they were never there to begin with.

It is remarkable how often we are warned in God's Book about the illicit abuse of our God-given sexuality. It isn't easy being sexually pure today. Then again, as we read these warnings, doesn't it become clear that it has never been easy? Ours is a time and culture that seems drunk with sex. It is everywhere, all around us. Most people find it exceedingly difficult to live one day without the lures of illicit sexuality making themselves prominently known in some way. For most, it's probably more difficult to avoid what God describes as evil than it is to find it.

All the more reason, then, to read these divine warnings carefully. Maybe you've read them dozens of times. Maybe you've preached through them. But calm your spirit, sharpen your focus, and read them again as if you had stumbled across them for the very first time. They are breathed-out by God (2 Tim 3.16–17). They deserve your utmost respect and serious attention.

"You have heard that it was said, 'You shall not commit adultery.' But I say to you that everyone who looks at a woman with lustful intent has already committed adultery with her in his heart. If your right eye causes you to sin, tear it out and throw it away. For it is better that you lose one of your members than that your whole body be thrown into hell. And if your right hand causes you to sin, cut it off and throw it away. For it is better that you lose one of your members than that your whole body go into hell." (Matt 5.27–30)

Let marriage be held in honor among all, and let the marriage bed be undefiled, for God will judge the sexually immoral and adulterous. (Heb 13.4)

Now the works of the flesh are evident: sexual immorality, impurity, sensuality, idolatry, sorcery, enmity, strife, jealousy, fits of anger, rivalries, dissensions, divisions, envy, drunkenness, orgies, and things like these. I warn you, as I warned you before, that those who do such things will not inherit the kingdom of God. (Gal 5.19–21)

Put to death therefore what is earthly in you: sexual immorality, impurity, passion, evil desire, and covetousness, which is idolatry. On account of these the wrath of God is coming. (Col 3.5–6)

For this is the will of God, your sanctification: that you abstain from sexual immorality; that each one of you know how to control his own body in holiness and honor, not in the passion of lust like the Gentiles who do not know God. (1 Thes 4.3–5)

The body is not meant for sexual immorality, but for the Lord, and the Lord for the body. (1 Cor 6.13)

But among you there must not be even a hint of sexual

immorality, or of any kind of impurity, or of greed, because these are improper for God's holy people. (Eph 5.3, NIV)

Therefore, since Christ suffered in his body, arm yourselves also with the same attitude, because he who has suffered in his body is done with sin. As a result, he does not live the rest of his earthly life for evil human desires, but rather for the will of God. For you have spent enough time in the past doing what pagans choose to do—living in debauchery, lust, drunkenness, orgies, carousing and detestable idolatry. (1 Pet 4.1–3, NIV)

Flee from sexual immorality. Every other sin a person commits is outside the body, but the sexually immoral person sins against his own body. (1 Cor 6.18)

For the commandment is a lamp and the teaching a light,
    and the reproofs of discipline are the way of life,
to preserve you from the evil woman,
    from the smooth tongue of the adulteress.
Do not desire her beauty in your heart,
    and do not let her capture you with her eyelashes;
for the price of a prostitute is only a loaf of bread,
    but a married woman hunts down a precious life.
Can a man carry fire next to his chest
    and his clothes not be burned?
Or can one walk on hot coals
    and his feet not be scorched?
So is he who goes in to his neighbor's wife;
    none who touches her will go unpunished.
People do not despise a thief if he steals
    to satisfy his appetite when he is hungry,
but if he is caught, he will pay sevenfold;
    he will give all the goods of his house.
He who commits adultery lacks sense;
    he who does it destroys himself. (Prov 6.23–32)

For the lips of a forbidden woman drip honey,
> and her speech is smoother than oil,
but in the end she is bitter as wormwood,
> sharp as a two-edged sword. (Prov 5.3–4)

Let us cast off the works of darkness and put on the armor of light. Let us walk properly as in the daytime, not in orgies and drunkenness, not in sexual immorality and sensuality, not in quarreling and jealousy. But put on the Lord Jesus Christ, and make no provision for the flesh to gratify its desires. (Rom 13.13–14)

Drink water from your own cistern,
> flowing water from your own well.
Should your springs be scattered abroad,
> streams of water in the streets?
Let them be for yourself alone,
> and not for strangers with you.
Let your fountain be blessed,
> and rejoice in the wife of your youth,
> a lovely deer, a graceful doe.
Let her breasts fill you at all times with delight;
> be intoxicated always in her love.
Why should you be intoxicated,
> my son, with a forbidden woman
> and embrace the bosom of an adulteress?
For a man's ways are before the eyes of the LORD,
> and he ponders all his paths.
The iniquities of the wicked ensnare him,
> and he is held fast in the cords of sin.
He dies for lack of discipline,
> and because of his great folly he is led astray.
> > (Prov 5.15–23)

If I am separated from God for all eternity, it will be because I chose to ignore the signposts, acting as if they were never there to begin with.

Core Questions

1. In Matthew 5.28, what does Jesus mean by "lustful intent"? In what way does "lustful intent" lead to committing adultery in the heart?

2. What sort of wickedness and perversion falls under the broad description of "sexual immorality"?

3. Paul writes in 1 Thessalonians 4.3, "For this is the will of God, your sanctification." What is sanctification and how is a person sanctified?

4. In your own words, what does Paul mean in 1 Corinthians 6.13?

5. In 1 Corinthians 6.18, Paul writes, "Every other sin a person commits is outside the body, but the sexually immoral person sins against his own body." What does this mean?

6. In Proverbs 5.3–4, what is meant by the dark promise that, in the end, the forbidden woman will be "bitter as wormwood"?

seven

A Time to Fight, and a Time to Run

"Now Joseph was handsome in form and appearance."[10] That is how the scene of temptation is set for us in Genesis 39.6. If you're familiar at all with Joseph's story, you know that at this point in his life, he is hundreds of miles away from home, having been sold by his own brothers as a worthless slave. Whatever he does in the distant land of Egypt, odds are, not one member of his family will ever find out. He's not married. That means he's free, right? Free to do whatever he wants. After all, who will ever know or even care anyway, especially when we remember the position Joseph now occupies in the house of a man named Potiphar, the captain of Pharaoh's guard.

Joseph found favor in [Potiphar's] sight and attended him, and [Potiphar] made him overseer of his house and put him in charge of all that he had.... So he left all that he had in Joseph's charge, and because of him he had no concern about anything but the food he ate. (Gen 39.4, 6)

Talk about freedom! Joseph's got boat loads. In many respects, he's his own boss. He can do whatever he wants in relative obscurity and ease. It would certainly have been easy to believe that there were finally nothing but blue skies and smooth waters ahead. And if anyone deserved the benefits and luxuries that came with the package, it was clearly Joseph.

It would not be long, however, before temptation reared its alluring head and Joseph would find himself in the midst of a serious battle. "After a time his master's wife cast her eyes on Joseph and said, 'Lie with me'" (Gen 39.7). There it is—an open, seductively engraved invitation. Can't you hear the seeds of fantasy and rationalization that would quite naturally bounce around within your mind? "Who will ever know? What will it hurt? I deserve this. She's the one who approached me. It's not that big of a deal. Just this once. I won't let it go too far."

Had Joseph's mind dwelt on those excuses, he would have succumbed to sexual temptation. But Joseph's mind was centered elsewhere.

"My Mind Is Already Made Up"

That's Rule #1 in the battle for integrity. Genesis 39.8 tells us that Joseph "refused." His mind had already been made up. The answer was "no." Later that same day, the answer would be "no." The answer would be "no" tomorrow. As far as Joseph was concerned, it was always going to be "no." With his whole heart he had already made up his mind. He wasn't going to allow himself the luxury of conflicting standards. He wouldn't give in to the temptations to reason, "I'll say 'no' for now, but 'maybe' later. I'll say 'no' to going all the way, but 'yes' to something a little more innocent. I'll say 'no' to this woman, but who knows about the next?"

Learn that lesson from Joseph! If you and I have any hope of surviving and ultimately winning the war for our souls, here is a lesson we must learn. Make up your mind right now! Dare to stand like Joshua, having chosen beforehand whom you will serve (Josh 24.15). Make up your mind as to what you will and will not do before the temptation hits.

That's what Job did when it came to sexual temptation. "I have made a covenant with my eyes," he said in Job 31:1; "how then could I gaze at a virgin?" To paraphrase, Job's mindset was,

> My eyes and I have already sat down and discussed the issue. We've come to an agreement. We're already on the same page. Through the course of the day, I may happen to see a lovely young lady, but I will not take the opportunity to gaze at her. I refuse to allow myself the luxury of making up my mind on a case-by-case, woman-by-woman basis. My eyes and my mind already understand what is and is not appropriate. The answer is "*no!*"

Why take such a hard and fast stand? Remember, Job had been richly blessed with material goods. "He possessed 7,000 sheep, 3,000 camels, 500 yoke of oxen, and 500 female donkeys, and very many servants, so that this man was the greatest of all the people of the east" (Job 1.3). Job was in a position to enjoy whatever his heart could desire. But he was also humble and honest enough to recognize the consequences of giving in to sexual immorality.

> "What would be my portion from God above
>   and my heritage from the Almighty on high?
> Is not calamity for the unrighteous,
>   and disaster for the workers of iniquity?
> Does not he see my ways
>   and number all my steps?" (Job 31.2–4)

In other words, "Even though I have bountiful physical blessings, what can I expect from my heavenly Father if I do not live as a person of godly character?" Rather,

"Let me be weighed in a just balance, and let God know my integrity!" (Job 31.6) "My mind is already made up!"

Is yours? Is your answer already "no"?

"Some Things Don't Belong To Me"

Here's our second line of defense against sexual temptation. What can you say when approached in some inappropriate way by a member of the opposite sex? She makes it obvious that you've caught her attention. He grows progressively bolder in his flirting. She "suddenly" shows up at very awkward times and seems to enjoy the awkwardness. He's relentless. She begins to push the limits. You never know when the next confrontation could come and you begin to dread the very thought of the possibilities.

Welcome to Joseph's world. Potiphar's wife "spoke to Joseph day after day," tempting him "to lie beside her or to be with her" (Gen 39.10). Notice carefully her tactics. Unable to persuade him to yield in her initial attempts, Potiphar's wife decides to assault Joseph with the temptation to compromise. "If you won't be with me, at least lie *beside* me."

Have you ever been tempted in that way? With seemingly innocent, little steps? Nothing too dramatic. "We won't go all the way. We won't actually have intercourse. It's just a little kiss. It's nothing more than a brush of skin on skin. What's the harm in just making out? What will it hurt if we just take off our clothes and lie beside each other? Is oral sex really that big of a deal?"

The temptation to compromise is real. It's powerful. It's deadly. I may enter into a confrontation with the determination to refuse, but I quickly reach the point where I must say something. What will it be? Words of integrity and strength, or words of compromise?

How did Joseph handle this volatile situation? We know "he refused," but what did he actually say?

> "Behold, because of me my master has no concern about anything in the house, and he has put everything that he has in my charge. He is not greater in this house than I am, nor has he kept back anything from me except yourself, because you are his wife." (Gen 39.8–9)

Take the time to appreciate Joseph's inner strength. He's not a man who doubts himself. He knows who he is, and he's not ashamed of it. Some men naturally morph into the equivalent of a third grader when tempted by a seductive woman. Not Joseph. In the midst of a tantalizing struggle, we get the impression that he speaks with authority.

But notice also Joseph's sense of moral balance. "Am I important? Yes! Have I been given great responsibilities? Absolutely. Are there a number of perks that come with my position? Without a doubt. Does that mean I can do whatever I want? Not for a moment!"

"Nor has he kept back anything from me except yourself, because you are his wife" (Gen 39.9). Take that example to heart! The fact that you've been blessed with eyes doesn't mean you have the right to look. The fact that you've been blessed with feet doesn't mean you have the right to go wherever you want. The fact that God has created you to naturally yearn for a physical relationship with a member of the opposite sex doesn't mean you have the right to act in whatever way you desire. There are some things that don't belong to you!

You don't have the sexual right to a married person other than your spouse. Joseph realized that. The only person on the face of the earth who had any kind of sexual rights to that woman was Potiphar, her husband. "Let marriage be held in honor among all, and let the marriage bed be undefiled, for God will judge the sexually immoral and adulterous" (Heb 13.4). If a person is married to someone else, he or she is off-limits. Period.

You don't have the right to do whatever you would like with a single person. Just because both parties aren't married doesn't mean they're free to act in whatever way their fleshly passions dictate. Sex with a married person is referred to as *adultery*, but the Bible also condemns sex between unmarried people as *fornication* or *sexual immorality*. Remember how inappropriate sexual behavior tops the cautionary list on several New Testament occasions:

> Now the works of the flesh are evident: sexual immorality, impurity, sensuality, idolatry, sorcery, enmity, strife, jealousy, fits of anger, rivalries, dissensions, divisions, envy, drunkenness, orgies, and things like these. I warn you, as I warned you before, that those who do such things will not inherit the kingdom of God. (Gal 5.19–21)

> Put to death therefore what is earthly in you: sexual immorality, impurity, passion, evil desire, and covetousness, which is idolatry. On account of these the wrath of God is coming. (Col 3.5–6)

> For this is the will of God, your sanctification: that you abstain from sexual immorality; that each one of you know how to control his own body in holiness and honor, not in the passion of lust like the Gentiles who do not know God. (1 Thes 4.3–5)

Is the person in whom you're interested still single? Wonderful! Just remember that you don't have a sexual right to them until you've married them. Period.

You don't have the right to sexually fantasize about *any* person who is not your spouse. What did Jesus say about the "Look-just-as-long-as-you-don't-touch" philosophy?

> "You have heard that it was said, 'You shall not commit adultery.' But I say to you that everyone who looks at a woman with lustful intent, has already committed adultery with her in his heart." (Matt 5.27–28)

Remember, just because you've been blessed with eyes doesn't mean you have the right to look. Men, if you look at any woman other than your wife with lust in your heart, you've sinned. Women, if you look at any man other than your husband with lust in your heart, you've sinned. Period.

As soldiers of the cross, now is the time to clearly define the boundaries and to recognize that some things just don't belong to us. We live in a world of traps and temptations on every hand. The examples of those in the high places of our society who have compromised their values in this regard are innumerable. Tragically, even those who have been a part of the Lord's church for decades are not immune. The battle comes to our doorstep daily.

The sexual relationship enjoyed by a man and woman is a beautiful thing. To demonize it is to disparage a divinely created and sanctioned joy of human existence. But the man or woman who does not realize and respect the fact that our Creator has regulated the joys associated with sex is a fool skipping along the pathway to hell. Sex as God envisioned always involves one man and one woman within the bonds of marriage.

"This Is A Sin Against God"

"How then can I do this great wickedness and sin against God?" (Gen 39.9). There's our third rule of engagement in the battle for physical and mental purity. Remember, Joseph is hundreds of miles away from home. What are the odds of his father ever finding out about his indiscretion? In his current position, why wouldn't he be able to arrange the circumstances so that no one would find out? And if no one finds out, what's the big deal?

Let's allow David, a man who learned this timeless truth the hard way, to answer that question for all time.

O Lord, you have searched me and known me!
You know when I sit down and when I rise up;
    you discern my thoughts from afar.
You search out my path and my lying down
    and are acquainted with all my ways.
Even before a word is on my tongue,
    behold, O Lord, you know it altogether.
You hem me in, behind and before,
    and lay your hand upon me.
Such knowledge is too wonderful for me;
    it is high; I cannot attain it.
Where shall I go from your Spirit?
    Or where shall I flee from your presence?
If I ascend to heaven, you are there!
    If I make my bed in Sheol, you are there!
If I take the wings of the morning
    and dwell in the uttermost parts of the sea,
Even there your hand shall lead me,
    and your right hand shall hold me.
If I say, "Surely the darkness shall cover me,
    and the light about me be night,"

Even the darkness is not dark to you;
> the night is bright as the day,
> for darkness is as light with you. (Psa 139.1–12)

You can't afford to overlook or forget this truth. As you step on the deadly land mines of fornication or adultery, it not only affects you and the person with whom you sin, it's an affront to the Almighty himself who knows exactly what you've done.

Long ago, the prophet Habakkuk affirmed the fact that our Lord is "of purer eyes than to see evil and cannot look at wrong" (Hab 1.13). It makes him nauseous. God is the forgiving Father of the "prodigal son" who selfishly demands his portion of the family inheritance, travels into a far country and wastes all of his blessings on wild living, allowing his father's heritage to be "devoured with prostitutes" (Luke 15.11–32). Our holy Creator graciously enables rebellious human beings who have mocked and spat in his Son's face to overcome their slavery to corruption. As Peter wrote, "the Lord is not slow to fulfill his promise as some count slowness, but is patient toward you, not wishing that any should perish, but that all should reach repentance" (2 Pet 3.9).

Far too often, however, our Father is forced to watch as one of his own, having "escaped the defilements of the world," becomes "again entangled in them and overcome" (2 Pet 2.20–22). You can't hide from the Almighty. He sees. He knows. Whether you're the overseer of a rich man's house in Egypt, or in the backseat of a car with your date on Friday night, or working overtime in a dark office with no one but your secretary, or in a lonely hotel room miles away from home, God sees. God knows.

"Sometimes The Bravest Thing You Can Do Is Run"

But one day, when he went into the house to do his work
and none of the men of the house was there in the house,
she caught him by his garment, saying, "Lie with me."
(Gen 39.11–12)

The great struggle between the lusts of the flesh and
honorable integrity had reached its climax. No one else
was in the house. Potiphar's wife had lost her patience.
She intended to take what she wanted, and take it at that
very moment. She physically grabbed hold of Joseph, "but
he left his garment in her hand and fled and got out of the
house" (Gen 39.11–12).

We don't generally commend soldiers for their
strength and courage when they run away as the battle
reaches its boiling point, but this is a different kind of
battle against a different kind of Enemy. Remember, "We
do not wrestle against flesh and blood, but against the
rulers, against the authorities, against the cosmic powers
over this present darkness, against the spiritual forces of
evil in the heavenly places" (Eph 6.12)

The last resort in your battle against sexual impurity
is this: sometimes the bravest thing you can do is run.
Isn't that what Paul was trying to convey in 1 Corinthians
6.18 when he wrote, "Flee from sexual immorality. Every
other sin a person commits is outside the body, but the
sexually immoral person sins against his own body." It's
worth noting that the word we have translated *flee* is
pheugo in Greek, a verb in the present tense that implies a
constant, habitual running away. "Run away from sexual
sin! Always run! And keep running as you run! Don't
look back!"

Don't forget this last point from Joseph's powerful
example. Some of the land mines we run across in the

battlefield for our souls are most effectively defeated by constant opposition and persistent fighting. But, let's face it. The Lord's battle plan against the deadly traps of sexual immorality calls for holy retreat.

Is your secretary getting a little too close? "Do not desire her beauty in your heart, and do not let her capture you with her eyelashes" (Prov 6.25).

Is your Friday night date wanting to go farther than you know is appropriate? "Can a man carry fire next to his chest and his clothes not be burned?" (Prov 6.27).

Have you run across a dark treasure chest of sinful images online? "For the lips of a forbidden woman drip honey, and her speech is smoother than oil, but in the end she is bitter as wormwood, sharp as a two-edged sword" (Prov 5.3–4).

Is your next door neighbor doing everything she can to get your inappropriate attention? "Can one walk on hot coals and his feet not be scorched? So is he who goes in to his neighbor's wife; none who touches her will go unpunished" (Prov 6.28–29).

Does the lonely hotel room seem like it provides the perfect opportunity? "The eyes of the LORD are in every place, keeping watch on the evil and the good" (Prov 15.3).

Are the circumstances around you piling up to the point that you're not sure you can control yourself? "Flee youthful passions" (2 Tim 2.22).

Are you already in bondage to sinful sexual habits and rationalizing that it's not that big of a deal? "Do not be deceived: God is not mocked, for whatever one sows, that will he also reap. For the one who sows to his own flesh will from the flesh reap corruption, but the one who sows to the Spirit will from the Spirit reap eternal life" (Gal 6.7–8).

The great day of God is coming. On that day, you and I will stand before the same throne as Joseph and "God will bring every deed into judgment, with every secret thing, whether good or evil" (Eccl 12.14). Because of his steadfast integrity and courageous character, Joseph will be ready to stand. Will you?

Core Questions

1. Why is making your mind up about your code of conduct before temptation hits so vital to spiritual success?

2. In what ways do people act as though certain illicit enjoyments "belong" to them, when they really do not?

3. Have you ever been personally tempted to compromise as Joseph was?

4. How do people live when they buy into the "Look-just-as-long-as-you-don't-touch" philosophy? Why is this attitude unacceptable in the sight of God?

5. What are some practical ways that you can consistently remind yourself, "This is a sin against God"? Why are those consistent reminders so important?

6. Have you ever had to resort to "holy retreat" from a specific temptation? How must 1 Corinthians 6.18 continue to shape your defense against future temptations?

eight

Frustration Sets In

Here's the problem. If you've read this far, I'm guessing you already know what Jesus said in Matthew 5.27–30. Odds are, you didn't need me to recount Joseph's story of courageous integrity from Genesis 39. You can probably recite the details of that story on your own. You might have even taught a Bible class or preached a sermon from that text. And while it's always worthwhile to read wise proverbs about the dangers of temptation and the pitfalls of sexual immorality, you've heard them before, haven't you? And you even know that the great day of judgment is coming! You know that every secret thing is one day going to be revealed by the perfectly righteous, holy, all-seeing God of the universe.

I'm guessing if you've read this far, you already know. You are painfully aware of the fact that your personal battle with pornography doesn't hinge solely on the knowledge in your head. You're familiar with the Biblical facts. You've heard the statistics quoted. You've watched as other brothers and sisters in Christ made sorrowful confessions as penitent prisoners of the war against sexual immorality. You've seen the tears of heartbroken spouses. You've sat in a pew as the warning is repeatedly sounded to "cast off the works of darkness and put on the armor of light" (Rom 13.12). You know. And so we have to go deeper.

Imagine a great field of battle. Imagine being hunkered

down with your fellow kingdom soldiers. The sun has set, but the battle rages on. Explosions rattle your helmet and brighten the sky as if it were noon. The streaks of enemy bullets whizz by your head. Orders are being screamed up and down the line. You realize that this is what you have been trained to do. This is what Boot Camp was all about. This is where the battle is the hottest, where soldiers show their mettle. The war for your soul and the souls of those you love is raging.

Finally, after what seems to have been an eternity's worth of waiting, the time comes to crawl out of the trench and confront the enemy head-on. Your objective is clear: gain the high ground, whatever the cost. A trumpet sounds. The Word of God leads the charge beneath the banners of heaven, his blood-soaked robe trailing in the wind. Warriors of the kingdom of light—flanking you to the right and left as far as the eye can see—rise as one. You courageously climb to your feet with a shout. And as you take your first steps forward, you're shot in the back— right through your heart.

But that doesn't make sense! The enemy is in front of you! In panic and confusion, you muster everything you have to turn around and see the traitorous culprit. Just before your eyes close and you take your last breath, you get a glimpse of the heartbreaking truth: a mirror image of yourself. *You* have shot your own self in the back.

Just a nightmare? A meaningless daydream? Not according to Paul, a veteran of the battlefield who describes his own personal grief over sin in vivid detail:

> For we know that the law is spiritual, but I am of the flesh, sold under sin. For I do not understand my own actions. For I do not do what I want, but I do the very thing I hate. Now if I do what I do not want, I agree

with the law, that it is good. So now it is no longer I who do it, but sin that dwells within me. For I know that nothing good dwells in me, that is, in my flesh. For I have the desire to do what is right, but not the ability to carry it out. For I do not do the good I want, but the evil I do not want is what I keep on doing. Now if I do what I do not want, it is no longer I who do it, but sin that dwells within me.

So I find it to be a law that when I want to do right, evil lies close at hand. For I delight in the law of God, in my inner being, but I see in my members another law waging war against the law of my mind and making me captive to the law of sin that dwells in my members. Wretched man that I am! Who will deliver me from this body of death? (Rom 7.14–24)

There are times when the war is most intense within—a struggle to the death between my mind and my fleshly body. I know what is right. I know what the Commander demands. But I also know what I want, what I need, what makes me feel good. At times, the battle is so intense that I'm made to agonizingly scream with Paul, "Wretched man that I am!" Why do I continue to make the same mistakes? Why do I so easily compromise what I know to be right? Why do I betray myself and my God? Will I ever learn to stop shooting myself in the back? "Who will deliver me from this body of death?"

Your problem, just like Paul's before you, does not stem from a lack of knowledge, or a disagreement with the law, or even a lack of desire to do what is right. Your problem is that sin has taken up residence within. Your inner being delights in the law of God, but your flesh is waging war—war against what you intellectually know. And at some point, you, like Paul, turned the throne of your soul over to sin.

When sin is allowed to reign in a mortal body, it makes you obey its passions (Rom 6.12). When you present your members to sin as instruments for unrighteousness, sin will begin exercising dominion over you (Rom 6.14). When you surrender yourself as an obedient slave to sin, it will lead you all the way to death (Rom 6.16, 23).

Paul had been there. I have been there. So have you. Sometimes we win. Too often, however, we are absolutely defeated. One more Biblical example should make that point perfectly clear.

Core Questions

1. Why, if we know better, do we continue to sin?

2. How can you personally relate to the illustration of shooting yourself in the back?

3. "For I do not understand my own actions," Paul writes in Romans 7.15. "For I do not do what I want, but I do the very thing I hate." Have you ever been there? In what ways?

4. What do you make of Paul's statement in Romans 7.17?

5. In what way does your flesh wage war against the law of your mind?

6. How, if you surrender yourself as an obedient slave to sin, will it lead you all the way to death?

Even Those After God's Own Heart Can Be Devoured

David's heart is applauded and held up as a powerful example in both the Old and New Testaments. In 1 Samuel 13.13–14, King Saul was given a glimpse of his dark future by the prophet Samuel.

> "You have done foolishly. You have not kept the commandment of the LORD your God, with which he commanded you. For then the LORD would have established your kingdom over Israel forever. But now your kingdom shall not continue. The LORD has sought out a man after his own heart, and the LORD has commanded him to be prince over his people, because you have not kept what the LORD commanded you."

It's one thing to be described as a man after God's own heart when you are still very young. But even after his death, David is ascribed the same sort of honor. David's son, Solomon, is contrasted with his father in 1 Kings 11.4. "For when Solomon was old his wives turned away his heart after other gods, and his heart was not wholly true to the LORD his God, as was the heart of David his father."

In 1 Kings 14.8, God used Ahijah the prophet to tell

King Jeroboam that his kingdom would be torn from him, because "you have not been like my servant David, who kept my commandments and followed me with all his heart, doing only that which was right in my eyes."

In 1 Kings 15.3, the reign of King Abijam is summarized with these words: "He walked in the sins that his father did before him, and his heart was not wholly true to the LORD his God, as the heart of David his father."

Hundreds of years later, David's reputation continued to live on. In Acts 13.22, the apostle Paul reminded Jews in Antioch of how God raised up David to be the king of Israel, saying of him, "I have found in David the son of Jesse a man after my heart, who will do all my will."

Once you have finished your time on this earth, if your life could be summarized in the same way that Paul summarized David's life, you will have done well. "For David, after he had served the purpose of God in his own generation, fell asleep and was laid with his fathers and saw corruption" (Acts 13.36). Abraham has fourteen chapters of the Bible dedicated to his life. Joseph also has fourteen. Jacob has eleven. Elijah has ten. David? Sixty-six chapters with fifty-nine references to his life in the New Testament. And yet, he was not some sort of an ethereal, super-saint. Yes, David was a "man after God's own heart." But don't overlook those first three letters. David was a *man*. And even David, when he was not sober-minded and watchful, could be devoured by the Adversary of our souls.

Second Samuel 11.1–2 documents the sad details for us:

> In the spring of the year, the time when kings go out to battle, David sent Joab, and his servants with him, and all Israel. And they ravaged the Ammonites and besieged Rabbah. But David remained at Jerusalem.

It happened, late one afternoon, when David arose from his couch and was walking on the roof of the king's house, that he saw from the roof a woman bathing; and the woman was very beautiful.

In that moment, David was faced with a choice. You know this sort of choice well, don't you? Will your eyes linger? Will you allow what you see to saturate your mind? You know what the Spirit of God commanded in Philippians 4.8–9:

Finally, brothers, whatever is true, whatever is honorable, whatever is just, whatever is pure, whatever is lovely, whatever is commendable, if there is any excellence, if there is anything worthy of praise, think about these things. What you have learned and received and heard and seen in me—practice these things, and the God of peace will be with you.

You know, without any shadow of a doubt, that to mentally dwell where your flesh yearns to dwell is not honorable. Those things that are percolating in your mind are neither just nor pure. There are so many external, enticing elements of this situation which seem lovely, but you know (deep down you *know!*) that the whole thing is laced with lies. Your initial leanings are not commendable. There is no excellence in where this could lead. Nothing about this encounter is worthy of praise.

As a redeemed child of the heavenly Father, you are the heir of a thrilling promise. Practice what is right, and the God of peace will be with you. And yet, you would rather, in that moment, mock your Father, spurn his promise, and drink a tall glass of filthy toilet water.

Blessed is the man who remains steadfast under trial, for when he has stood the test he will receive the crown of life, which God has promised to those who love him. Let no one say when he is tempted, "I am being tempted by God," for God cannot be tempted with evil, and he himself tempts no one. But each person is tempted when he is lured and enticed by his own desire. Then desire when it has conceived gives birth to sin, and sin when it is fully grown brings forth death. (Jas 1.12–15)

This is exactly the path that David, a man after God's own heart, was willing to take on that spring evening.

David sent and inquired about the woman. And one said, "Is not this Bathsheba, the daughter of Eliam, the wife of Uriah the Hittite?" So David sent messengers and took her, and she came to him, and he lay with her. (2 Sam 11.3–4)

David and Bathsheba committed adultery. A child was conceived. A cover-up was devised. Dark plans were foiled. David got desperate. He plotted murder. Uriah, Bathsheba's husband, was placed in a situation where death was almost guaranteed. He lost his life, and so did a number of other valiant soldiers. Wives became widows. Children became orphans. David, in his sin-hardened heart, breathed a sigh of relief. "But the thing that David had done displeased the Lord" (2 Sam 11.4–27).

Core Questions

1. What does "after God's own heart" mean?

2. What set David apart from men like Solomon, Jeroboam, and Abijam?

3. Was it wrong for David to see Bathsheba bathing?

4. If not, when did sin first enter into the picture?

5. In the moment of temptation, why can no one say, "I am being tempted by God"?

6. How does desire conceive and give birth to sin? What does full-grown sin look like? And how does it ultimately bring forth death?

ten

Counting the Cost

One of the most sobering things a person can do is to count the cost of being defeated on this front of the war for the soul. It's certainly a Biblical principle. In the context of warnings against sexual immorality, remember the wise questions of Proverbs 6.27–28:

> Can a man carry fire next to his chest
> and his clothes not be burned?
> Or can one walk on hot coals
> and his feet not be scorched?

Wisdom encourages us to stand at the trailhead of this dark, forbidden pathway and think before we take another step—at what cost will this fleeting pleasure come? Certainly David, if he were able to speak with us, would beg us to count the cost! Begin walking this trail, and elements of your life will be unalterably burned. Decide to follow this path, and some of the most precious aspects of your existence will be forever scorched.

Take a moment and use this blank space to count your personal cost. Commit fornication or adultery, and what aspects of your life will be impacted? Allow yourself to become ensnared in an addiction to pornography, and what sort of collateral damage will be inflicted? If that secret you've been keeping for a long time finally becomes known, what areas of your life will be affected?

As I look down this pathway and count the possible cost, the price is steep. Fail to stand steadfast on the sexual immorality front of the war for my soul, and the ensuing damage could be devastating.

- I will have turned my back on the only sacrifice suitable to atone for my sins.

- I will have reopened the door to a fearful expectation of judgment.

- I will have spurned the very Son of God.

- I will have profaned the blood of the covenant by which I was sanctified.

- I will have outraged the Spirit of grace.

- I will have declared myself an enemy of the Almighty.

- I will have exchanged the pure holiness of my heavenly Father for the fleeting and foolish passions of my former ignorance.

- I will have compromised my new identity in Christ.

- I will have become a prisoner of war to sin and corruption.

- I will have destroyed countless dreams for the future as a preacher and author.

- I will have shattered elements of my influence with others that has taken years to build.

- I will have made a mockery of the love Christ expects of me as a husband.

- I will have demolished years of trust with my wife that might never be rebuilt.

- I will have caused indescribable pain and embarrassment to my best friend.

- I will have threatened the dynamics of sexual intimacy for the rest of my marriage.

- I will have emotionally scarred my daughters beyond comprehension. The impact my sexual sins could have on their own sexuality, self-esteem, and their view of men is immeasurable.

- I will have endangered healthy relationships with my sisters in Christ in countless ways.

- I will be forced to acknowledge that I foolishly learned nothing from the examples of those who have fallen in the same ways before me.

- I will have shamed my physical family.

- I will have shamed my spiritual family.

- I will almost certainly have forfeited my opportunity to preach where I am currently located and might never enjoy another opportunity again.

- I will have severely disappointed and hurt those I have helped lead to Christ.

- I will have undermined every good thing I ever did in the minds of many.

- I will have brought great satisfaction to the Adversary of my soul.

- I will have dishonored the glory of God, which I was created and redeemed to reflect.

And on and on the list could go. If you didn't do so on the previous page, I would seriously encourage you to make a similar, very personal list. Do so, and the wisdom of Proverbs 7.21–23 will become frighteningly real.

With much seductive speech she persuades him;
> with her smooth talk she compels him.
All at once he follows her,
> as an ox goes to the slaughter,
or as a stag is caught fast
> till an arrow pierces its liver;
as a bird rushes into a snare;
> he does not know that it will cost him his life.

eleven

God's Steadfast Love is Better Than Life

And so why do we sin? Having counted the cost, why would we choose to do what we know to be wrong? Why would we be willing to gamble so much for so little?

Simply put, we prefer other things, other people, and other pleasures more than we prefer God. And that is precisely why something as addictive as pornography is so difficult to defeat. We can readily identify the shortcomings, we can easily pinpoint the bad habits, we can drill encouraging slogans into our heads, we can establish a variety of accountability safeguards ... and continue to be sifted as wheat! How? Why? We have failed to accurately diagnose the root of the problem.

Pornography is a problem, but it is not *the* problem. Pornography is a sinful symptom of the problem. Masturbation is a problem, but it is not *the* problem. Masturbation is an ugly manifestation of the problem. The adulterous affair is certainly a problem, but it is not *the* problem. The adulterous affair is a wicked reflection of the problem. *The* problem is treasuring other things, other people, and other pleasures more than we treasure God.

Take a moment to carefully read and truly meditate upon Psalm 51. The subtitle reads, "To the choirmaster. A Psalm of David, when Nathan the prophet went to him, after he had gone in to Bathsheba."

Have mercy on me, O God,
    according to your steadfast love;
according to your abundant mercy
    blot out my transgressions.
Wash me thoroughly from my iniquity,
    and cleanse me from my sin!

For I know my transgressions,
    and my sin is ever before me.
Against you, you only, have I sinned
    and done what is evil in your sight,
so that you may be justified in your words
    and blameless in your judgment.
Behold, I was brought forth in iniquity,
    and in sin did my mother conceive me.
Behold, you delight in truth in the inward being,
    and you teach me wisdom in the secret heart.

Purge me with hyssop, and I shall be clean;
    wash me, and I shall be whiter than snow.
Let me hear joy and gladness;
    let the bones that you have broken rejoice.
Hide your face from my sins,
    and blot out all my iniquities.
Create in me a clean heart, O God,
    and renew a right spirit within me.
Cast me not away from your presence,
    and take not your Holy Spirit from me.
Restore to me the joy of your salvation,
    and uphold me with a willing spirit.

Then I will teach transgressors your ways,
    and sinners will return to you.
Deliver me from bloodguiltiness, O God,
    O God of my salvation,
    and my tongue will sing aloud of your righteousness.
O Lord, open my lips,
    and my mouth will declare your praise.

For you will not delight in sacrifice, or I would give it;
    you will not be pleased with a burnt offering.
The sacrifices of God are a broken spirit;
    a broken and contrite heart, O God, you will not
       despise.

Do good to Zion in your good pleasure;
    build up the walls of Jerusalem;
then will you delight in right sacrifices,
    in burnt offerings and whole burnt offerings;
    then bulls will be offered on your altar.

Isn't it interesting what *isn't* in Psalm 51? David had committed adultery, lied, manipulated, and murdered. And yet, in his classic psalm of confession, not one of those sins is specifically identified. Bathsheba isn't even named. Neither is Uriah. Why is that? Because David's transgressions were serious symptoms of the greatest ailment of all—not treasuring God above every other person, pleasure, and thing. Look at these key sections again:

I know my transgressions,
    and my sin is ever before me.
Against you, you only, have I sinned
    and done what is evil in your sight.

Create in me a clean heart, O God,
    and renew a right spirit within me.
Cast me not away from your presence,
    and take not your Holy Spirit from me.
Restore to me the joy of your salvation,
    and uphold me with a willing spirit.

Like Paul after him, David's sin did not stem from ignorance. David's shortcoming was not the result of a long-held, deep-seeded disagreement with the laws of God. He was a man after God's own heart! But on that night, David wanted illicit sexual gratification more than he wanted God. In the days that followed, David guarded his sinful secret more than he guarded his covenant with God. When the situation grew desperate, David feared the awful truth being revealed more than he feared God. When backed into a corner, David demonstrated more of a willingness to shed innocent blood than to honestly and penitently cast himself before the feet of the God who already knew what David had done. David was exactly right when he confessed, "I have sinned against the Lord" (2 Sam 12.13).

And the same is true for us. "The body is not meant for sexual immorality, but for the Lord, and the Lord for the body" (1 Cor 6.13). "Put on the Lord Jesus Christ, and make no provision for the flesh, to gratify its desires" (Rom 13.14). "God has not called us for impurity, but in holiness. Therefore whoever disregards this, disregards not man but God, who gives his Holy Spirit to you" (1 Thes 4.7–8).

Every day we are faced with decisions, opportunities, tests, and trials. We know what God has said, but will we supplement our knowledge with integrity? We know what God expects, but will we fortify Biblical truth with personal character? We hear preaching about righteousness, self-control and the coming judgment on Sundays, but will we reinforce the facts with faith on Mondays?

Are the blessings that flow from your connection with God more gratifying than the sinful images that can flow through your connection to the Internet? That is the question! If not, you will find yourself enslaved to pornography. Late at night, when everyone else is in bed, is the urge to pray stronger than the tugs of sin on the garment of your flesh? If not, sin will seize an opportunity to deceive you. "Blessed are the pure in heart, for they shall see God" (Matt 5.8). Does that blessed assurance of seeing God mean more to you in the moment than self-centered, self-gratifying masturbation? If not, you will continue to do the very thing you hate.

Until you treasure God as more precious than pornography, you will continue to be in bondage to pornography. Until you cherish God as more satisfying than masturbation, you will continue to be enslaved to masturbation. Until the pain of being separated from God is greater than the pain of repentance, you won't give up your sin.

And so God invites you to personally accept the challenge of Psalm 34. Make these words your own. Turn the verbs like *bless, magnify, exalt, sought, cried, fear, taste,* and *see* into the verbs that will control your own conduct.

> I will bless the LORD at all times;
>> his praise shall continually be in my mouth.
> My soul makes its boast in the LORD;
>> let the humble hear and be glad.
> Oh, magnify the LORD with me,
>> and let us exalt his name together!
>
> I sought the LORD, and he answered me
>> and delivered me from all my fears.
> Those who look to him are radiant,
>> and their faces shall never be ashamed.
> This poor man cried, and the LORD heard him
>> and saved him out of all his troubles.
> The angel of the LORD encamps
>> around those who fear him, and delivers them.
>
> Oh, taste and see that the LORD is good!
>> Blessed is the man who takes refuge in him!
> Oh, fear the LORD, you his saints,
>> for those who fear him have no lack!

The young lions suffer want and hunger;
    but those who seek the Lord lack no good thing.

Come, O children, listen to me;
    I will teach you the fear of the Lord.
What man is there who desires life
    and loves many days, that he may see good?
Keep your tongue from evil
    and your lips from speaking deceit.
Turn away from evil and do good;
    seek peace and pursue it.

The eyes of the Lord are toward the righteous
    and his ears toward their cry.
The face of the Lord is against those who do evil,
    to cut off the memory of them from the earth.
When the righteous cry for help, the Lord hears
    and delivers them out of all their troubles.
The Lord is near to the brokenhearted
    and saves the crushed in spirit.

Many are the afflictions of the righteous,
    but the Lord delivers him out of them all.
He keeps all his bones;
    not one of them is broken.
Affliction will slay the wicked,
    and those who hate the righteous will be
        condemned.
The Lord redeems the life of his servants;
    none of those who take refuge in him will be
        condemned.

In the moment of temptation, which taste buds will you gratify? The seductively-engraved invitation of illicit indulgence entices you to taste and see.

For the lips of a forbidden woman drip honey,
    and her speech is smoother than oil,

but in the end she is bitter as wormwood,
   sharp as a two-edged sword. (Prov 5.3–4)

How desperately we must tell ourselves in the moment of trial, "You are being *lied* to! There is a sweeter alternative. There is a superior satisfaction!"

Oh taste and see that the LORD is good!
   Blessed is the man who takes refuge in him!
Oh, fear the LORD, you his saints,
   for those who fear him have no lack!
The young lions suffer want and hunger;
   but those who seek the LORD lack no good
      thing.

God invites us to delight in him. Savor him. Crave more than bits of intellectual knowledge *about* him. Fearfully avoid the temptation to confine him to the margins of your life. Refuse to act as though you can use him in whatever ways you choose and whenever you find it convenient. Taste and see that the LORD is good!

How refreshing and liberating are the words of David in Psalm 63.1–3:

O God, you are my God; earnestly I seek you;
   my soul thirsts for you;
my flesh faints for you,
   as in a dry and weary land where there is no water.
So I have looked upon you in the sanctuary,
   beholding your power and glory.
Because your steadfast love is better than life,
   my lips will praise you.

An intimate relationship with God is better than the highest sexual high. Purposeful communion with him is more enjoyable than any earthly gratification. A consistent walk with him is more thrilling than any fleeting deviance. His refining fellowship is more exhilarating than anything this world will ever offer. Forsake the mirages and flee to him! Respond to his compassionate call in Psalm 81.13–16:

> "Oh, that my people would listen to me,
>> that Israel would walk in my ways!
> I would soon subdue their enemies
>> and turn my hand against their foes.
> Those who hate the LORD would cringe toward him,
>> and their fate would last forever.
> But he would feed you with the finest of the wheat,
>> and with honey from the rock I would satisfy you."

Quit shoveling the feces of sin into your mind and joyfully fill your soul with the bread of heaven (John 6.33–51). Walk away from the toilet water of iniquity and drink deeply from the living water that has the power to satisfy your greatest thirst (John 4.10; 7.37–38).

Sin will continue to promise gratification, but it is lying to you. It is lying to me. Oh, how it lies to us! Confront your temptations and conquer them with the superior satisfaction which flows only from a deep, rich, intimate connection with God. Make your prayer the prayer of Moses in Psalm 90.12–14:

> So teach us to number our days
>> that we may get a heart of wisdom.
> Return, O LORD! How long?
>> Have pity on your servants!
> Satisfy us in the morning with your steadfast love,
>> that we may rejoice and be glad all our days.

Temptations will come, but let them come. God is more powerful. God is more satisfying.

No temptation has overtaken you that is not common to man. God is faithful, and he will not let you be tempted beyond your ability, but with the temptation he will also provide the way of escape, that you may be able to endure it. (1 Cor 10.13)

Core Questions

1. How have you personally shown in the past that you prefer other things, other people, and other pleasures more than you prefer God?

2. Why is making David's words in Psalm 51.4 so pivotal to being forgiven of your sins?

3. Until you treasure God as more precious than pornography, you will continue to be in bondage to pornography. Why?

4. Until you cherish God as more satisfying than masturbation, you will continue to be enslaved to masturbation. Why?

5. Until the pain of being separated from God is greater than the pain of repentance, you won't give up your sin. Why?

6. Practically speaking, what does it mean to "taste and see that the LORD is good" (Psa 34.8)?

twelve

The Fruit of a Broken and Contrite Heart

There are two types of grief associated with secret sin that has been discovered. First, there is what the apostle Paul calls "worldly grief" (2 Cor 7.10). Worldly grief is sorrow and regret that I feel because I was caught. I didn't want my sins to come to light. I didn't intend to face my sins. I will endure whatever I must endure for the moment, but my heart has not been cut to the core. My conscience has not been pricked. My affections have not been touched. And so, given enough time and the right opportunity, I will return to wallow in the filth of my sin.

> For whatever overcomes a person, to that he is enslaved. For if, after they have escaped the defilements of the world through the knowledge of our Lord and Savior Jesus Christ, they are again entangled in them and overcome, the last state has become worse for them than the first. For it would have been better for them never to have known the way of righteousness than after knowing it to turn back from the holy commandment delivered to them. What the true proverb says has happened to them: "The dog returns to its own vomit, and the sow, after washing herself, returns to wallow in the mire." (2 Pet 2.20–22)

Worldly grief allows sin to continue reigning in my

mortal body. I will continue to live as a slave to the passions of my flesh. Sin will keep on exercising cruel dominion over me. The only thing I have to look forward to in such a state is death.

But thanks be to God that there is another path—the path of "godly grief." We have talked about some difficult things in this book. As you have stared into the mirror of God's word, perhaps you see the need for some very real, grueling, demanding changes in your ways of thinking and living. All God-glorifying change that will ultimately reconcile you to him is initiated by hearing hard truths that produce "godly grief." Consider what Paul wrote in his second letter to the Corinthians as he reflects on the first letter they had received.

> For even if I made you grieve with my letter, I do not regret it—though I did regret it, for I see that that letter grieved you, though only for a while. As it is, I rejoice, not because you were grieved, but because you were grieved into repenting. For you felt a godly grief, so that you suffered no loss through us.
>
> For godly grief produces a repentance that leads to salvation without regret, whereas worldly grief produces death. For see what earnestness this godly grief has produced in you, but also what eagerness to clear yourselves, what indignation, what fear, what longing, what zeal, what punishment! At every point you have proved yourselves innocent in the matter. (2 Cor 7.8–11)

Anyone can mouth the words, "I repent!" But it is another thing entirely to bear what John the Baptist called "fruit in keeping with repentance" (Matt 3.8). "The word of God is living and active, sharper than any two-edged sword, piercing to the division of soul and spirit, of joints and marrow, and discerning the thoughts and intentions of the heart" (Heb 4.12). And when God's word is allowed to teach, reprove, and correct a receptive and honest heart, godly sorrow will be the natural result.

> Cleanse your hands, you sinners, and purify your hearts, you double-minded. Be wretched and mourn and weep. Let your laughter be turned to mourning and your joy to gloom. Humble yourselves before the Lord and he will exalt you. (Jas 4.8–10)

With those truths in mind, make sure that the next few minutes are free of distraction. Calm your spirit. Focus your mind. Open your heart, and carefully read the words of David in Psalm 32.

> Blessed is the one whose transgression is forgiven,
>   whose sin is covered.
> Blessed is the man against whom the LORD counts
>   no iniquity,
>   and in whose spirit there is no deceit.
>
> For when I kept silent, my bones wasted away
>   through my groaning all day long.
> For day and night your hand was heavy upon me;
>   my strength was dried up as by the heat of
>   summer.
>
> I acknowledged my sin to you,
>   and I did not cover my iniquity;
> I said, "I will confess my transgressions to the
>   LORD,"
>   and you forgave the iniquity of my sin.
>
> Therefore let everyone who is godly
>   offer prayer to you at a time when you may
>   be found;

surely in the rush of great waters,
>they shall not reach him.
You are a hiding place for me;
>you preserve me from trouble;
>you surround me with shouts of deliverance.

I will instruct you and teach you in the way you
>should go;
>I will counsel you with my eye upon you.
Be not like a horse or a mule, without understanding,
>which must be curbed with bit and bridle,
>or it will not stay near you.

Many are the sorrows of the wicked,
>but steadfast love surrounds the one who
>trusts in the LORD.
Be glad in the LORD, and rejoice, O righteous,
>and shout for joy, all you upright in heart!

Core Questions

1. In your own words, describe "worldly grief"?

2. Why will I continue in my sin if my heart has not been cut to the core?

3. How is "godly grief" different from "worldly grief"?

4. In what way does godly grief produce a repentance that leads to salvation without regret?

5. As you evaluate your own standing before God, what will bearing fruit "in keeping with repentance" look like?

6. How can you personally relate to David's words in Psalm 32?

thirteen

It's Time to Walk Down Another Street

One of my favorite poems about temptation and maturity is called, *There's a Hole in My Sidewalk*, by Portia Nelson.

Chapter 1
I walk down the street.
There is a deep hole in the sidewalk.
I fall in.
I am lost.
I am helpless.
It isn't my fault.
It takes forever to find a way out.

Chapter 2
I walk down the same street.
There is a deep hole in the sidewalk.
I pretend I don't see it.
I fall in again.
I can't believe I am in this same place.
But it isn't my fault.
It still takes a long time to get out.

Chapter 3
I walk down the same street.
There is a deep hole in the sidewalk.
I see it is there.
I still fall in ... it's a habit.

But my eyes are open.
I know where I am.
It is my fault.
I get out immediately.

Chapter 4
I will walk down the same street.
There is a deep hole in the sidewalk.
I walk around it.

Chapter 5
I walk down another street.

In Philippians 3.18–21, Paul lamented the fact, with tears in his eyes, that many walk as enemies of the cross of Christ.

> Their end is destruction, their god is their belly, and they glory in their shame, with minds set on earthly things. But our citizenship is in heaven, and from it we await a Savior, the Lord Jesus Christ, who will transform our lowly body to be like his glorious body, by the power that enables him even to subject all things to himself.

It's time to be honest. It's time for some authentic, fearless self-evaluation. What god am I serving? If the god of some first-century Philippians was their belly, who am I to believe that I might not be guilty of the same sort of thing? To what or whom has my allegiance been pledged?

It's time to take personal responsibility. It's time to purge. It's time to mature. It's time to stop flirting with the desires of the flesh. It's time to quit seeing just how close to the edge I can get. It's time to move on. It's time to taste and see that the Lord is good. It's time to be enraptured by what I have seen, and tasted, and savored. It's time to be gloriously broken by God and remolded, all the way down to my very core.

"Come, let us return to the LORD;
>   for he has torn us, that he may heal us;
>   he has struck us down, and he will bind us up."
>   (Hos 6.1)

It's time to wholeheartedly and unashamedly imitate the holiness of God. It's time to walk down another street.

Core Questions

1. How have you modeled the different chapters of Portia Nelson's poem in the past?

2. Where have you gone, or what have you chosen to be involved in, that has turned out to be a serious hole in the sidewalk of your life?

3. Why must so many of us fall into the same hole numerous times before we are willing to change our ways?

4. Why is it so tempting to repeatedly "walk down the same street," despite our knowledge of the danger ahead?

5. Practically speaking, in what areas of life do you need to walk down a completely different street?

6. Are there ways that God has torn you in the past, that he might heal you? Can you think of specific instances where he has struck you down, that he may bind you up?

fourteen

Hacking Agag to Pieces

"I see in my members another law waging war against the law of my mind" (Rom 7.23). "Your passions are at war within you" (Jas 4.1). "Abstain from the passions of the flesh, which wage war against your soul" (1 Pet 2.11).

War is upon and around and within you, whether you acknowledge it or not. The good news is, "There is therefore now no condemnation for those who are in Christ Jesus.... We are more than conquerors through him who loved us" (Rom 8.1, 37). But the same context that contains God's promise for us, contains God's expectation of us. "Brothers, we are debtors, not to the flesh, to live according to the flesh. For if you live according to the flesh you will die, but if by the Spirit you put to death the deeds of the body, you will live" (Rom 8.12–13).

If you would stand and remain on the side of ultimate victory, you must make a wholehearted declaration of all-out, relentless, holy war against your sin. Enough compromise. Make war! No more procrastination. Make war! Refuse the rationalizations. Make war!

> There is a mean streak to authentic self-control.... Self-control is not for the timid. When we want to grow in it, not only do we nurture an exuberance for Jesus Christ, we also demand of ourselves a hatred for sin.... The only

possible attitude toward out-of-control desire is a declaration of all-out war.... There is something about war
that sharpens the senses.... You hear a twig snap or the
rustling of leaves and you are in attack mode. Someone
coughs and you are ready to pull the trigger. Even after
days of little or no sleep, war keeps us vigilant.[11]

With these things in mind, consider what has been
preserved for us in 1 Samuel 15. It's a lengthy account,
but worth your time and attention.

And Samuel said to Saul, "The LORD sent me to anoint
you king over his people Israel; now therefore listen to
the words of the LORD. Thus says the LORD of hosts, 'I
have noted what Amalek did to Israel in opposing them
on the way when they came up out of Egypt. Now go
and strike Amalek and devote to destruction all that they
have. Do not spare them, but kill both man and woman,
child and infant, ox and sheep, camel and donkey.'"

So Saul summoned the people and numbered them
in Telaim, two hundred thousand men on foot, and ten
thousand men of Judah. And Saul came to the city of
Amalek and lay in wait in the valley. Then Saul said
to the Kenites, "Go, depart; go down from among
the Amalekites, lest I destroy you with them. For
you showed kindness to all the people of Israel when
they came up out of Egypt." So the Kenites departed
from among the Amalekites. And Saul defeated the
Amalekites from Havilah as far as Shur, which is east of
Egypt. And he took Agag the king of the Amalekites
alive and devoted to destruction all the people with the
edge of the sword. But Saul and the people spared Agag
and the best of the sheep and of the oxen and of the fat-
tened calves and the lambs, and all that was good, and
would not utterly destroy them. All that was despised
and worthless they devoted to destruction.

The word of the LORD came to Samuel: "I regret that I have made Saul king, for he has turned back from following me and has not performed my commandments." And Samuel was angry, and he cried to the LORD all night. And Samuel rose early to meet Saul in the morning. And it was told Samuel, "Saul came to Carmel, and behold, he set up a monument for himself and turned and passed on and went down to Gilgal." And Samuel came to Saul, and Saul said to him, "Blessed be you to the LORD. I have performed the commandment of the LORD." And Samuel said, "What then is this bleating of the sheep in my ears and the lowing of the oxen that I hear?" Saul said, "They have brought them from the Amalekites, for the people spared the best of the sheep and of the oxen to sacrifice to the LORD your God, and the rest we have devoted to destruction." Then Samuel said to Saul, "Stop! I will tell you what the LORD said to me this night." And he said to him, "Speak."

And Samuel said, "Though you are little in your own eyes, are you not the head of the tribes of Israel? The LORD anointed you king over Israel. And the LORD sent you on a mission and said, 'Go, devote to destruction the sinners, the Amalekites, and fight against them until they are consumed.' Why then did you not obey the voice of the LORD? Why did you pounce on the spoil and do what was evil in the sight of the LORD?" And Saul said to Samuel, "I have obeyed the voice of the LORD. I have gone on the mission on which the LORD sent me. I have brought Agag the king of Amalek, and I have devoted the Amalekites to destruction. But the people took of the spoil, sheep and oxen, the best of the things devoted to destruction, to sacrifice to the LORD your God in Gilgal." And Samuel said,

> "Has the LORD as great delight in burnt offerings
> and sacrifices,
> as in obeying the voice of the LORD?

Behold, to obey is better than sacrifice,
    and to listen than the fat of rams.
For rebellion is as the sin of divination,
    and presumption is as iniquity and idolatry.
Because you have rejected the word of the Lord,
    he has also rejected you from being king."

Saul said to Samuel, "I have sinned, for I have transgressed the commandment of the Lord and your words, because I feared the people and obeyed their voice. Now therefore, please pardon my sin and return with me that I may worship the Lord." And Samuel said to Saul, "I will not return with you. For you have rejected the word of the Lord, and the Lord has rejected you from being king over Israel." As Samuel turned to go away, Saul seized the skirt of his robe, and it tore. And Samuel said to him, "The Lord has torn the kingdom of Israel from you this day and has given it to a neighbor of yours, who is better than you. And also the Glory of Israel will not lie or have regret, for he is not a man, that he should have regret." Then he said, "I have sinned; yet honor me now before the elders of my people and before Israel, and return with me, that I may bow before the Lord your God." So Samuel turned back after Saul, and Saul bowed before the Lord.

Then Samuel said, "Bring here to me Agag the king of the Amalekites." And Agag came to him cheerfully. Agag said, "Surely the bitterness of death is past." And Samuel said, "As your sword has made women childless, so shall your mother be childless among women." And Samuel hacked Agag to pieces before the Lord in Gilgal.

Then Samuel went to Ramah, and Saul went up to his house in Gibeah of Saul. And Samuel did not see Saul again until the day of his death, but Samuel grieved over Saul. And the Lord regretted that he had made Saul king over Israel.

Core Questions

1. How have you made compromises, procrastinated, and rationalized your sin in the past? Why must those things stop immediately if you are to conquer your sin?

2. Summarize God's initial instructions to King Saul in 1 Samuel 15.

3. How did Saul deviate from God's expectations?

4. In what ways have you made the same types of excuses and rationalizations that Saul made to Samuel?

5. How must Samuel's words in 1 Samuel 15.22–23 shape your thinking?

6. "Samuel hacked Agag to pieces before the LORD" (1 Sam 15.33). Specifically speaking, what sins must you hack to pieces in order to be acceptable to God?

fifteen

Equipped for the Battles Ahead

Following Jesus is not a settle-in-and-live-at-peace-with-the-world-the-way-it-is kind of lifestyle. With Christ comes war.

> We do not wrestle against flesh and blood, but against the rulers, against the authorities, against the cosmic powers over this present darkness, against the spiritual forces of evil in the heavenly places. (Eph 6.12–13)

The hosts of wickedness are powerful, but they cannot defeat the will of our Creator. God's book ends with this assurance: with allegiance to Christ will come absolute victory; loyalty to the Enemy will bring certain destruction. The outcome of the war over our souls has already been decided. As the Spirit of God told Jehoshaphat and his subjects, "Do not be afraid and do not be dismayed at this great horde, for the battle is not yours but God's" (2 Chron 20.15).

And so the only variable in this equation is you. God is faithful. Have you chosen to dedicate yourself to Him in sincerity and faithfulness? God is a fortress, a very present help in time of need. Have you hidden your heart and your life in the care and protection of the ultimate Victor? If not, why take another unprepared, unconsecrated step?

Be vigilant. "Keep your heart with all vigilance, for from it flow the springs of life" (Prov 4.23). "Be sober-minded; be watchful. Your adversary the devil prowls around like a roaring lion, seeking someone to devour" (1 Pet 5.8). Begin your day with prayer. Saturate your day with prayer. End your day with prayer. "Lead me not into temptation, but deliver me from evil."

Commit to being a person of radical integrity. Make up your mind right now. Dare to stand like Joshua, having chosen in advance whom you will serve (Josh 24.15). Unashamedly pledge your allegiance before another temptation hits. Make a covenant with your eyes and stick to it, regardless of the cost (Job 31.1).

Fight for the joy of your salvation. Hunger and thirst for those superior satisfactions that can sever the roots of the lies of this world. Take honest inventory. What enhances your joy in God? What robs you of your joy in God? Then, base your daily decisions on your God-breathed knowledge and your Christ-shaped character.

Die daily. Put to death what is earthly in you: sexual immorality, impurity, passion, evil desire, and covetousness, which is idolatry. Remind yourself each day that on account of those ugly things the wrath of God is coming. Put all these things away: anger, wrath, malice, slander, and obscene talk from your mouth. Do not lie, seeing that you have put off the old self with its practices and have put on the new self, which is being renewed in knowledge after the image of its creator (Col 3.5–10). Get violent against your shortcomings. Relentlessly attack the footholds of Satan and your flesh with the strength that God supplies.

Be honest. Following Christ can, at times, be a lonely walk. More than ever before, however, technology can be used in good and constructive ways to encourage and be encouraged. Use the people and resources at your disposal to fend off the discouragement of isolation. Honestly acknowledge and seek spiritual reinforcement for the areas of life where you are being defeated.

Be accountable. Tools of accountability—particularly for the fight against online temptations—are readily available; several of them are free. I have free software installed on every computer I use that monitors all Internet sites I visit. Anything deemed morally questionable or unacceptable is recorded and sent to the two e-mail addresses of my accountability partners twice a month. Accountability breeds integrity.

Be receptive to rebukes rooted in truth. It took Nathan and his strong confrontation of David to wake David from his sin-induced slumber and his hardness of heart (2 Sam 12.1–15). Odds are, the same will be true, at times, for us. Be mature enough to ask God to provide friends and acquaintances as bold as Nathan. Periodically remind yourself that you are capable of being "the wanderer" of James 5.19–20. "My brothers, if anyone among you wanders from the truth and someone brings him back, let him know that whoever brings back a sinner from his wandering will save his soul from death and will cover a multitude of sins." Thank God for those who have brought you back from the brink in the past, and be humble enough to thank them as well.

Preach to yourself. Memorize the words of Psalm 42.5. Recite them forcefully and regularly to your own soul, especially in moments of temptation. "Why are you cast down, O my soul, and why are you in turmoil within me? Hope in God; for I shall again praise him, my salvation and my God."

Remember the warning of James 3.1. "Not many of you should become teachers, my brothers, for you know that we who teach will be judged with greater strictness." Those who teach the truth should consistently remind themselves that there will be no excuses for any sort of immorality on the great day when God brings "every deed into judgment, with every secret thing, whether good or evil" (Eccl 12.14).

Don't be afraid to retreat. Remember! Sometimes the bravest thing you can do is run. "Flee from sexual immorality" (1 Cor 6.18).

Celebrate victories. Unashamedly and frequently exult in what God has done in your life. Say with David, "The LORD is my rock and my fortress and my deliverer, my God, my rock, in whom I take refuge, my shield, and the horn of my salvation, my stronghold. I call upon the LORD, who is worthy to be praised, and I am saved from my enemies" (Psa 18.2–3).

Learn from defeats. Everyone falls. Every man and every woman suffers defeat from time to time. But people of integrity make the effort and take the time to learn so that they might avoid repeating the mistakes of the past. Ruthlessly analyze the weak spots in your spiritual armor. When and where are you most vulnerable to temptation? Sharpen your spiritual senses to the triggers that have led to past downfalls. Only the fool ignores such things.

Take the time to refresh yourself. "Finally, brothers, whatever is true, whatever is honorable, whatever is just, whatever is pure, whatever is lovely, whatever is commendable, if there is any excellence, if there is anything worthy of praise, think about these things" (Philippians 4:8). It is so very easy to become so consumed with our daily obligations that we fail to adequately feed and refresh ourselves. Don't allow your own soul to wither out of personal negligence. A beat-down, worn-out, shriveled soul plus a sudden, seductive temptation will end in spiritual disaster more often than not.

Recognize and destroy the idolatry in your life. Sex is a gift, a wonderful blessing of our Creator. But the gift of sex is not greater than the Giver. Enjoy his good gift in the way he has prescribed. But even then, don't be so enamored with the gift that you fail to give complete allegiance to the Giver. Such is idolatry, defection, and betrayal against the One who matters most of all.

> To him who is able to keep you from stumbling and to present you blameless before the presence of his glory with great joy, to the only God, our Savior, through Jesus Christ our Lord, be glory, majesty, dominion, and authority, before all time and now and forever. Amen. (Jude 24–25)

I'm praying for you. Please pray for me. May our heavenly Father be gracious to us and daring in his use of us as we grow to be more fully conformed to the image of his Son (Rom 8.29). He alone makes known the path of life. In his presence there is fullness of joy. At his right hand are pleasures forevermore.

notes

1. "Carnage At Antietam, 1862," EyeWitness to History, www. eyewitnesstohistory.com.

2. www.covenanteyes.com. The complete 19-page report with all 99 sources cited is available at http://www.covenanteyes.com/blog/2010/01/06/updated-pornography-statistics/

3. Damon Brown. Weblog: *damonbrown, Music, Tech and Sex.* "PCs in Ecstasy: The Evolution of Sex in PC Games (Computer Games Magazine)." Web. 20 Jan. 2010. <http://damonbrown.net/2006/05/01/pcs-in-ecstasy-the-evolution-of-sex-in-pc-games-computer-games-magazine/>.

4. Rich Frank. "Naked Capitalists: There's no Business like Porn Business." *New York Times,* 20 May 2001, *New York Times Magazine.* Web. 20 Jan. 2010. <http://www.nytimes.com/2001/05/20/magazine/20PORN.html>.

5. Timothy C. Morgan. "Porn's Stranglehold." *Christianity Today Magazine,* 7 March 2008. Web. 20 Jan. 2010.
<http://www.christianitytoday.com/ct/2008/march/20.7.html>

6. Gary R. Brooks. *The Centerfold Syndrome: How Men Can Overcome Objectification and Achieve Intimacy with Women.* Jossy-Bass Pub 1995. SF, CA.

7. Patrick F. Fagan, Ph.D. *The Effects of Pornography on Individuals, Marriage, Family, and Community.* Web 20 Jan. 2010. <http://www.frc.org/pornography-effects>.

8. Tim Challies. "Sexual Detox." Web. 20 Jan. 2010. <http://www.challies.com/archives/christian-living/sexual-detox-the-e-book.php>

9. C.S. Lewis, *The Screwtape Letters*. Simon & Schuster, 1996. Letter 12.

10. This chapter is adapted from Jason Hardin's *Boot Camp: Equipping Men with Integrity for Spiritual Warfare*. DeWard Publishing, 2009. 97–109.

11. Edward Welch. "Self-Control: The Battle Against 'One More.'" *The Journal of Biblical Counseling* 19 (Winter 2001): 30.

Also By Jason Hardin

Boot Camp
*Equipping Men with Integrity
for Spiritual Warfare*

Boot Camp is where a soldier is
equipped for the battles ahead and
where he learns from the veterans
of previous wars. Boot Camp:
Equipping Men with Integrity for
Spiritual Warfare is the first volume in the new IMAGE series of
books for men by Jason Hardin. It
serves as a Basic Training manual
in the spiritual war for honor, integrity and a God-glorifying life.
237 pages, $13.99 (PB); $24.99
(HB).

"This is a great book to help us men live opposite of this
world's model of a man."

Stephen Arterburn
Best-Selling Author, including *Every Man's Battle*

"Jason focuses like a laser beam on a theme that has been the
defining passion of my own life for some years now. Writing
particularly, but not exclusively, for men, he urges us to lift our
vision to the extraordinary things that God can make possible
in us through His Son, Jesus Christ. Our problem is not that
we desire too much but that we settle for so little. I was stirred
deeply by this triumphant call to arms. Jason has that unique
combination of spiritual insight, emotional maturity, and liter-
ary zest that make a writer's work special. This is a must-read!
I will be impatient for the remaining volumes in the series!"

Gary Henry
Author of *Diligently Seeking God* and *Reaching Forward*

ALSO FROM DEWARD PUBLISHING:

Beneath the Cross: Essays and Relfections on the Lord's Supper
Jady S. Copeland and Nathan Ward (editors)

The Bible has much to say about the Lord's Supper. Almost every component of this memorial is rich with meaning—meaning supplied by Old Testament foreshadowing and New Testament teaching. The Lord's death itself is meaningful and significant in ways we rarely point out. In sixty-nine essays by forty different authors, Beneath the Cross explores the depths of symbolism and meaning to be found in the last hours of the Lord's life and offers a helpful look at the memorial feast that commemorates it. 329 pages. $14.99 (PB); $23.99 (HB).

Invitation to a Spiritual Revolution
Paul Earnhart

Few preachers have studied the Sermon on the Mount as intensively or spoken on its contents so frequently and effectively as the author of this work. His excellent and very readable written analysis appeared first as a series of articles in Christianity Magazine. By popular demand it is here offered in one volume so that it can be more easily preserved, circulated, read, reread and made available to those who would not otherwise have access to it. Foreword by Sewell Hall. 173 pages. $10.99 (PB)

The Slave of Christ
Seth Parr

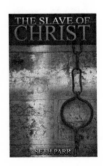

Immerse yourself in a place where sacrifice is reasonable, love and action are sensible, victory is guaranteed, and evangelism explodes. While the sacrifice of Jesus opens the door for us to Heaven, we must work to be conformed into His very image. In The Slave of Christ, uncover what biblical service means and how it can change your life. Energize your spiritual walk and awaken the servant within. 96 pags. $8.99 (PB)

Thinking Through Jeremiah
L.A. Mott

When Jesus came, some of his contemporaries thought that he was Jeremiah reincarnated. Yet many Bible students today know less about him than about a host of other Old Testament heroes. One who turns to commentaries for help will find that many of them are filled with complex discussions of strange Hebrew words and consideration of technical, critical questions with which most of us are totally unconcerned. A serious Bible student wishing to know Jeremiah and to understand his character, his preaching and his times will be grateful for L.A. Mott's Thinking Through Jeremiah. Foreword by Sewell Hall. 214 pages. $12.99 (PB)

The Growth of the Seed: Notes on the Book of Genesis
Nathan Ward

A study of the book of Genesis that emphasizes two primary themes: the development of the Messianic line and the growing enmity between the righteous and the wicked. In addition, it provides detailed comments on the text and short essays on several subjects that are suggested in, yet peripheral to, Genesis. 537 pages. $19.99. (PB)

Churches of the New Testament
Ethan R. Longhenry

Have you ever wondered what it would be like to be a Christian in the first century, to meet with the church in Philippi or Ephesus? *Churches of the New Testament* explores the world of first century Christianity by examining what Scripture reveals about the local churches of God's people. It examines background information about the geography and history of each city, as well as whatever is known about the founding of the church there. Centuries may separate us from the churches of the New Testament, but their examples, instruction, commendation, and rebukes can teach us today. 150 pages. $9.99 (PB)

DeWard's Heritage of Faith Library

The Man of Galilee
Atticus G. Haygood

Dr. Haygood's apologetic for the deity of Christ using Jesus Himself as presented by the gospel records as its chief evidence. This is a reprint of the 1963 edition. The Man of Galilee was originally published in 1889. Preface by Ferrell Jenkins and Homer Hailey. New preface by Dr. Dan Petty. 108 pages. $8.99 (PB).

Jesus and Jonah
J. W. McGarvey

McGarvey's defense of the historicity of the Biblical account of the book of Jonah based on Jesus' teaching about Jonah—which is the same as His teaching regarding the historicity of the rest of the Old Testament. This would indicate that Jesus either accepts all of it as historical or none of it as historical. Since the New Testament makes it plain that Jesus accepts the Old as historical, McGarvey argues that the denial of the Jonah story makes Jesus either a liar or a fool. New foreword by Dr. David McClister. 76 pages. $7.99 (PB).

Original Commentary on Acts
J. W. McGarvey

McGarvey's classic commentary on Acts, attractively re-typeset and added to our Heritage of Faith collection. 344 pages. $13.99 (PB).

Coming soon to the Heritage of Faith Library:

The Training of the Twelve
A.B. Bruce

A Treatise on the Eldesrhip
J.W. McGarvey

The Fourfold Gospel
J.W. McGarvey

Natural Theology
William Paley

The Lamb, The Woman and The Dragon
Albertus Pieters

*For a full listing of DeWard Publishing
Company books, visit our website:*

www.dewardpublishing.com

DEWARD
PUBLISHING COMPANY

CPSIA information can be obtained at www.ICGtesting.com
Printed in the USA
BVOW05s1746230414

351127BV00001B/13/P